What people are sa

The Anti-consume.

Katrina Townsend's experience of navigating from a consumerist world into one that enters the realms of spirituality is beautifully expressed in this book. Her writing is open and honest, humorous and thought-provoking and takes you along the journey to where one can find peace in both the self and the world. It's an ongoing process, as she demonstrates so well in this book, of reviewing and reflecting upon one's habits and, for some, addiction, and being able to come out with a real sense of breaking the cycle of wanting more, through learning to love what you have. In this we find spirituality, expressed in this book through the tradition of Druidry and its love of nature which guides us to live our lives according to that love. I highly recommend this book to everyone, Druids and Pagans, and people of all faiths and none. **Joanna van der Hoeven**, Director of Druid College and author of several books including *The Book of Hedge Druidry*, *The Hedge Druid's Craft* and *The Awen Alone: Walking the Path of the Solitary Druid*

The way Katrina writes is relatable and motivational, effortlessly mixing the spiritual with a humorous take on the more mundane aspects of life and showing how they're more connected than we might think. The book gave me a real sense of 'I can do this too'. It was engaging and felt like sitting down for tea and a chat with a good friend – I truly and thoroughly enjoyed it. **Isabelle Alexandra Louise**, Tarot reader, artist and sustainable fashion designer at Clove and Moon

I really enjoyed the journey Katrina takes us on – through her re-discovery of paganism and her relationship to community after taking a conscious step back from mindless consumerism. Her initial decision to take a spending break took on a life of its own, eventually evolving into a more informed way of looking at the world outside of her doorstep, deepening her relationships with her loved ones, and rekindling her spiritual relationship with the land she lives on, all over the course of a two-year period. I definitely think one of the best parts was being reminded of that infinite feeling of discovery at your fingertips that paganism can provide when you're starting out on your journey in earnest. It's something we can lose sight of over time, and it feels like a much-needed breath of fresh air as Katrina takes us along on her spiritual discovery culminating in a tangible relationship to her matron goddess.

Trinidy Patterson, proprietor of the HedgeWitch Haus, Occult writer, and Herbalist

Katrina Townsend's journey from hedonistic consumerism to a deep communion with nature makes for a fascinating and compelling read. She writes with engaging honesty as well as humour, delving into the wisdom and magic of our Celtic past to find her own truth in the modern world. Her story will resonate with anyone who has found solace in walking England's green lanes, or glimpsed an older reality in the contours of hill and hedgerow.

Jill Todd, author of *Echo of Bells*

The Anti-consumerist Druid

How I Beat My Shopping Addiction Through Connection With Nature

The Anti-consumerist Druid

How I Beat My Shopping Addiction Through Connection With Nature

Katrina Townsend

MOON BOOKS

Winchester, UK
Washington, USA

JOHN HUNT PUBLISHING

First published by Moon Books, 2022
Moon Books is an imprint of John Hunt Publishing Ltd., No. 3 East Street, Alresford
Hampshire SO24 9EE, UK
office@jhpbooks.net
www.johnhuntpublishing.com
www.moon-books.net

For distributor details and how to order please visit the 'Ordering' section on our website.

Text copyright: Katrina Townsend 2021

ISBN: 978 1 78904 519 2
978 1 78904 520 8 (ebook)
Library of Congress Control Number: 2021949916

A CIP catalogue record for this book is available from the British Library.

Design: Matthew Greenfield

UK: Printed and bound by CPI Group (UK) Ltd, Croydon, CR0 4YY
Printed in North America by CPI GPS partners

We operate a distinctive and ethical publishing philosophy in
all areas of our business, from our global network of authors to
production and worldwide distribution.

Contents

For Dai and the Spud

Acknowledgements

I owe so much to my dad and fellow author, Norman Townsend, who sadly passed away whilst this book was still a work in progress. Thank you, Dad, for your endless support, advice and encouragement. I miss you every day.

Thanks most of all to my husband 'Dai' for your support and total unflappability, and to my gorgeous Spudling for teaching me patience, perseverance, and the benefits of playing in the mud. Thanks, Mum, for raising me the way you did, I'm pretty happy with how I turned out and I hope you are too. I love you all and hope this book won't embarrass you too much.

(Hello, dear family and friends who are reading this to support me! I am very grateful! I look forward to having many awkward conversations with you once you've finished this book and all illusions of my normality have been shattered.)

Much love and gratitude also to 'Topaz', 'Bel', 'Alice', 'Ana', Trinidy and Isabelle for your great kindness in reading and advising on early drafts of this book. A thousand blessings upon you!

Thanks also to Moon Books for giving me this opportunity.

Introduction

For much of my life, I have been what is politely termed an 'overshopper'. Addiction is a strong word, and I have no wish to minimise the struggles of others, but I can say with alacrity that throughout my teens and twenties my shopping behaviour held many of the hallmarks of addiction, a fact that was only brought home to me when I tried to stop, and couldn't.

There are many excellent books by overshoppers who have kicked the habit. The concept of a shopping ban – no unnecessary purchases for a self-defined period of time, usually between 30 days and one year – has become a hot topic on YouTube channels and minimalist lifestyle blogs, as more and more of us come to realise that we're hooked, and it's doing serious damage to our finances, our relationships, our mental and emotional health, our creativity, and even the planet. However, my path to breaking the habit and escaping the clutches of overshopping led me down a road rather less travelled.

My journey to becoming an anti-consumerist suburban Druid began in 2019, when I started keeping a daily journal to document my progress on a year-long shopping ban, intended to get my frantic spending under control before I ruined our family finances beyond repair. I hoped that writing down my thoughts each day would help me to unravel the thorny tangle of complicated emotions, insecurities, attachments and conditioning I had around shopping (and not shopping) which had led me to this point, as well as holding myself accountable as I struggled to learn how to manage my spending. I'm glad that I did decide to write that journal, which I have been keeping diligently ever since, as now I am able to share with you my triumphs, tips and failures, as well as everything I learned about myself and about the society we live in as I attempted to quit shopping, live a greener life, and sidestep the mindless consumerism that had dominated my existence for far too long.

Shopping bans may be a ubiquitous topic nowadays as those of us in the 'developed' global North – home of affluence, abundance, and, of course, advertising – come to terms with the devastating planet-wide effects of our extreme overconsumption, but whilst there are hundreds of people vlogging, blogging and writing about their personal battles with consumerism, I have not yet stumbled across anyone else whose desire to quit shopping has led them to explore Paganism, and then to Druidry!

Likewise, whilst I keep up with Druid blogs and podcasts, and have immersed myself in studying Druidry, I have yet to find anyone talking about environmentally-related topics such as consumerism, wastefulness and shopping addiction from an inside perspective – that of someone whose life has been devoted (and I don't use that term lightly) to the cult of the consumer. The process of becoming involved with this earth-based spiritual path, with its roots sunk deep into the bedrock of history, folklore and mythology, has entailed a radical personal transformation, which I will tell you more about as we proceed.

Suffice to say, if you are an overshopper, I've been in your shoes. You don't have to become a Druid to overcome shopping addiction, but I hope that many of the principles by which I now live, such as connection with – reverence for – nature, building strong and supportive communities, caring for the earth and its ecosystem (of which, let's not forget, we are a part) and being true to your innermost self, will help you consider a different way of living.

This is not a book about Druidry. This is a book about how I stopped overconsumption consuming me, and on that journey discovered a connection with nature that led to my becoming a student of Druidry. This is a book about how the beliefs and practices of Druidry helped me to rebuild a more authentic, creative way of living, and to tread more lightly upon the earth.

If you are a Druid, then first and foremost, I apologise! In

Druidry terms, I am a rank beginner. Most people who write books about Druidry are or have been Chief this or Arch that, or are often otherwise sage and venerable people with many years of experience and study under their robes. Me? Well, not so much. What I hope to be able to share instead is a different perspective on this tradition; a sense of how studying Druidry has changed and enriched my life. And if you too are a beginner would-be Druid, then welcome! Perhaps we can stumble along together, exploring the relevance of ancient myth in our fast-paced, maddening modern times.

The first part of this book is the embarrassing part – the story of my shopping addiction, and my struggle to overcome it. Whilst writing, it was all too easy to imagine friends, family, and the worldly-wise Druid authors and bloggers I have come to admire sucking in their breath and shaking their heads at my shallow nature and profligate ways! But it's hard to show the transformation in me and in my life – my re-enchantment, if you will – without showing you, in all honesty, where I came from and how I got to this point.

The second half of my tale is rather different from the first. A new awareness of nature had begun working change upon me, and the end result was nothing I could have predicted when I first set out upon my attempt to go a year without shopping. If you picked this book up looking for discussion of Druidry, this is where you'll find it – so please do bear with me, it's in here!

I also intend to touch on many other topics, such as body image, minimalism, social media, ethical consumption, environmentalism and fast fashion, and you will see how all of these interrelated threads have influenced and affected – well, me, for a start, but also our society at large and the way many of us in the comparatively wealthy global North consume today. This is not a self-help book or a Paganism 101 – although I can recommend both of those in the Further Reading section at the back! – I suppose more than anything it's a sort-of memoir, but it is my hope that in my struggles (both the large and the petty) you may see echoes of your own, and that those things that have helped and guided me may also help and guide you.

My story begins where so many of us start our journeys: at rock bottom.

Part I
Come for the Shopaholism...

Chapter 1

Identity Crisis

The day my fiancé Dai and I went to give notice of our intent to marry, I had to tell him that I'd spent the maternity allowance my employer had paid me over the last ten months whilst I was at home with our baby boy. That was the money that was supposed to give us a buffer, to help us through the next couple of years until the little one started nursery and I could go back to work part time.

Instead, I had a wardrobe bursting at the seams with clothes, hundreds of perfume samples, thousands of unread books and magazines... There were charges on my bank statement that I couldn't identify, but I knew they weren't fraudulent. I'd just shopped so much that I'd forgotten what I'd bought. Even visitors commented on the frequency of the deliveries turning up with more, more, more. Checking my bank balance felt like staring down the barrel of a loaded weapon. Something had to give.

Salvation was at hand in the form of holiday pay which would arrive in my account in three months' time. It wouldn't make up for the savings I had blown, but it would stabilise my finances and give us a chance to find our feet. Meanwhile, I had to stop shopping.

No one could ever accuse me of being a fashionista. As a child I constantly wore socks with my sandals, and to be honest I probably still would if my mother hadn't eventually put her foot down. The best word you could use to describe my outerwear collection is 'sensible'. And yet the greatest wear and tear on my wallet for over a decade was clothing. My preoccupation with trying to improve the way I looked was costing me a fortune.

Since my early teens I had developed a tendency to try to

buy myself a sense of identity. Hours, days, weeks of my life vanished on Pinterest, Instagram, Tumblr, the endless scroll of 'inspiration', seeking the photo or quote or One True Garment that would somehow express perfectly every nuance of my essence, encapsulate everything I wanted strangers to know about me. I bounced from subculture to subculture, and gradually my own taste was lost in the morass, subsumed by a tide of images and vague ideas of fashion 'rules'.

I had gone from being a carefree child cheerfully wearing bobbly hand-knitted cardigans, to an anxious adult paralysed in Primark. Facing a rack of clothes in what was supposed to be yet another last-ditch wardrobe overhaul, in which I cleared out a large chunk of the clothes I had and replaced them, thereby creating a New Me who would somehow have it together, I realised that I didn't know which of the selection of T-shirts before me I actually *liked*.

My childhood had by and large been unspoilt and simple; reading, writing, drawing, making things for my own pleasure and at my own pace. I hoped to recapture this freedom of mind and abundance of spirit, rather than spending every waking moment fixated on things whose only true value to me was the fact that I didn't already own them.

Emotionally, I was exhausted from comparing myself to every woman I saw. I had style mood boards coming out of my ears, but what looked good in a Milan street style photo and what seemed reasonable to wear for a dash round Aldi when the baby had a tummy bug just didn't gel.

I hated the way I looked. I hated that I could no longer trust myself with money. I wasn't raised to be a spendthrift – quite the opposite! I hated that I didn't know who I was any more, and now that the money was quite simply gone – wasted – I had to accept that I could never solve this identity crisis by throwing more cash at it.

The concept of the shopping ban has seen an unlikely surge in popularity in recent years, in various guises, such as cosmetics obsessives trying to use up ('pan') their existing hoards of products, to a simple thirty-day ban on clothes purchases to save a little money or enable a wardrobe edit, to the more seriously arduous no-spend year a la writer Michelle McGagh,[1] who cycled her jeans to smithereens on a spending-free holiday and endured twelve brave months of tap water in the pub. Or taking it to the next level altogether, journalist Mark Boyle, who gave up using money entirely for one year,[2] putting my comparatively simple challenge firmly in the shade. I may have found it a struggle to avoid the open doors and budget temptations of TK Maxx, but I didn't brew my own tea from foraged herbs or build a compost toilet.

With the rise of minimalism and Marie Kondo on the one hand, and an increased awareness of the threat of man-made climate change, caused in no small part by overproduction of consumer goods, on the other, the modern-day shopper is becoming more aware of the power of our money to create change, both within ourselves and the world at large. We are often encouraged to 'vote with our wallets' to promote sustainability in a society on the cusp of catastrophe, but it's only more recently that mainstream culture is beginning to take note of dissenting voices telling us that to avoid climate breakdown, the first thing we need to do is buy *less*.

A shopping ban is a way to press pause, to take stock of and appreciate all that we already have. During the last few years, I had several times attempted short shopping bans, and had discovered to my discomfort that I couldn't last a week. I discovered Canadian writer Cait Flanders,[3] who completed a two-year shopping ban, and my reaction was rage – I closed the tab, put her out of my mind, and chose not to investigate the shocking surge of anger I had felt.

But the idea had struck a chord, and now I realised I had no other options left. So I embarked on a quest not to shop for one whole year.

Shopping Ban Rules[4]

- No new clothes or accessories (unless something essential wears out beyond repair, or an unexpected black-tie event happens. Note: I have found that unexpected black-tie events generally do not happen)
- No new magazines, books or e-books (normally I wouldn't ban book buying as the acquisition of knowledge is a great thing, but in this first year I was buried under unread books, and as much as I wanted to support authors, my first priority was to save some cash)
- No new cosmetics – replacing used items only
- No housewares unless needed, e.g. a replacement
- Gifts are allowed
- "Experiential" purchases, e.g. eating out, are allowed

I started my first serious attempt at a shopping ban in May 2019. My son was seven months old; I was newly engaged and knee-deep in wedding plans. On maternity leave but with my maternity allowance finished, I was also broke.

Let me note here that I am aware of my privileged position. Dai was working full time; I was able to take maternity leave and stay at home to raise our child. Some remaining vestige of common sense had stopped me from continuing my credit card application, so, unlike many people who become overshoppers, I had avoided running into debt.

The first month of the ban was difficult. I wanted. I browsed. I longed. I scrolled. I chafed at the boundaries I had put on myself. My journal filled with lists – what I wanted to buy, what I could ask for for my birthday, what my wardrobe still needed to be 'complete'.

At this early juncture, my goals were still appearance-focused – I wanted this break from shopping to help me clarify my 'signature style', to allow my own true likes and dislikes to emerge from wherever they were buried. I also wanted to end the comparison game that was eroding my self-esteem – as far as I could tell, every woman, everywhere, was better dressed, happier in her skin, had better hair. I wanted to learn how to feel okay about just being me. But first I had to relearn who the heck I was.

I was not a born shopaholic. I was raised in a Hampshire village in the UK, somewhere on the borderline between rural life and suburbia, in the nineties, by a mother who still grew her own vegetables and sourced her cough remedies from the herb garden. I grew up playing outdoors in all weather, eating elderberries, nettles and beech nuts. My clothes were second-hand, my toys from boot sales and charity shops.

Introverted, bookish, with no understanding of or interest in fashions and fads, by the time I hit secondary school it was clear that I wasn't going to fit in. At fourteen I was bullied badly enough that my mum pulled me out of school, and I became home-educated.

In my early teens I started crash dieting and obsessively counting calories. My relationship with food and weight came to define the better part of a decade as I starved, binged, purged, exercised until I fainted, took diet pills and laxatives, and generally made my own life a misery.

When I discovered goth culture it became an obsession, an outlet – I started work at eighteen, and every paycheque went on Sisters of Mercy CDs, vampire novels and a slew of black clothing. Saving up my pocket money to buy a new outfit as a birthday treat morphed and grew into a collection of avidly maintained wish lists and lavish shopping sprees to Camden Market.

I got a job in a charity shop, and the floor of my room soon disappeared under mountains of stuff. My books overflowed from the shelves and then the desk. They were piled in every corner, collecting mug marks and dust. They were in crates under the bed, and when I moved house in my early twenties, I found I had multiple copies of the same book – I had so many I couldn't keep track, let alone keep up with reading them all (though I did my best)!

I had so many clothes it was almost impossible to get into my room. I had three wardrobes, all full to bursting, and eventually I started to colonize the spare room and the hallway as well. I never wore the same outfit twice, and was regularly up to forty minutes late for work because I wouldn't leave the house until my hair and make-up were perfect and I had taken a good enough 'outfit of the day' photo for my blog.

In my mind I was living the dream, but I wasn't saving any money and I was utterly fixated on the way I looked.

My blog became quite popular – it got me a regular slot writing for an American alternative magazine, occasional gifts and freebies, a decent amount of ad revenue, an interview with a nice lady from the Guardian, and a few very nice people coming up and asking for photos when I was out and about at gigs. I posted daily, sometimes as many as four times a day, and maintained a Facebook page, Twitter, Lookbook (anyone else still remember Lookbook?), YouTube channel, Pinterest and Tumblr connected to the blog as well.

When my fascination with all things goth started to wane, I felt confused and guilty. So much time, effort and money had gone into building this very public persona. The goth subculture, its emphasis on individuality and self-expression, had given me a place of belonging and something to focus on. For a good few years afterwards I stumbled from label to label trying to find a new niche where I could fit.

By the time I met my future fiancé, aged twenty-five, four

years after I eventually quit my career as a goth blogger, I had decided that being as conventionally attractive as possible was the main goal (no sense of identity + long-term relationship break-up + way too much social media = bizarre headspace and a skewed perception of what 'everyone else' is expecting of you) and to such an end I had amassed a vast new wardrobe, an array of cosmetic products to doctor every flaw, and appointments – bookings made, deposits paid – for a raft of varyingly intrusive cosmetic procedures (none of which I went through with, much to my relief now).

I considered myself recovered from disordered eating, but with hindsight I can see that my confidence had been damaged by the way I'd treated and talked to myself during those years, some of the situations I'd stayed in beyond all reason, and by the unrealistic standards I'd been setting. (I'm happy to say that this is much improved now, particularly over the past couple of years when I have drastically cut myself some slack with a great deal of support from Dai.)

Pregnancy and motherhood came as a further shock to my self-image. I was curvier than I had ever been, with new stretchmarks and unrecognizable boobs. New glasses, hormonal acne and an awkwardly grown out bob haircut meant that I barely knew the person in the mirror.

So I turned to the only solution I knew. I went shopping. By January 2019 I was spending hundreds of pounds on my tablet most nights while feeding the baby. I tried to stop, or at least to slow down, but it wasn't until I was almost out of money that I managed to apply the brakes. I didn't get a buzz from shopping any more, just a sense of panic, guilt and anxiety, and I knew it was time to (try to) go cold turkey.

I appreciate that people reading this who have not experienced shopping addiction may be appalled by my wastefulness and self-obsession. Hey, I'm not delighted either. It wasn't a pretty picture, at the time. Younger me had some underlying issues, but the behaviours visible on the surface were shallow, vain, and often selfish. I knew I had to tackle the problems head-on, but even so it took a long time and some serious hard work to break once and for all my association between spending money, and feeling a sense of identity, of self-worth. To know, at a bone-deep level, that I am not the way I look, and that I am not what I buy.

Day One of my first shopping ban – May 14th, 2019 – started badly. I had expected to feel Zen Master-pure, worthy and brimming with self-love, so of course the baby had a bad night, I screwed up my knitting pattern (oh, the horror) and I felt wretched, gross and crabby. My adjustment to motherhood had not been smooth, and occasionally I wondered if I could be depressed, but generally chalked it up to being flat-out tired and missing my pre-baby headspace and autonomy, a state I had been self-medicating with those huge shopping sprees on my tablet during the late-night feeds.

It was an eye-opener of a fortnight; I balked and struggled at every turn. I went through my bank statements from January to May and wrote down exactly what I'd spent on frivolous purchases – a deeply upsetting exercise, but a necessary one, after which I had a good cry in the shower and felt deeply ashamed for a long while. I came clean to Dai about the money I had wasted and how tight things now were. It was not a pleasant or a comfortable conversation, but he accepted the news with surprising calmness, though I felt terrible.

And yet, I was heartened. Each time I had previously attempted a shopping ban, by day three or four I'd discovered something I absolutely had to have, and given up. This time, I tried to minimise the amount of time I had to spend battling against myself and cut down on my online browsing. Physical shops, I simply avoided. I had come to see that sometimes in all my obsessive browsing I was merely looking for a fix. I was buying just to get the buzz that came with typing in my card number.

Thirty days is commonly the minimum length recommended for a shopping ban. Not as dramatic as a year-long challenge, but long enough to reset, to break free just a little from the unrelenting pursuit of more. Sure enough, by mid-June, I was starting to gain a clarity I had been missing.

In physical shops, it was usual for me to fall into what I thought of as 'the trance of greed', whereby I became so focused on buying that it was impossible for me to concentrate on anything else. If a companion tried to chat with me, I could feel my eyes darting past them, desperate to ensure I wasn't missing something I might want. I could hardly follow a conversation, and at times even became irritated or angry at being distracted from shopping.

With hindsight, the ubiquitousness of technology – and thereby marketing, via email offers, influencers, shoppable Instagram feeds and targeted ads – and its constant presence in my life had led to a constant, low-level trance of greed. When I wasn't shopping, I was thinking about shopping, planning purchases, creating moodboards to define my 'style concept' to help me decide what to buy next. I was absorbed by social media, permanently distracted by the shiny and new, reliant on the next thing, or the next, to fix the sense I had that I was lacking in some way. As I stopped shopping, my ability to concentrate increased. I found I was more patient, more alert, more interested. It was as though I had been hibernating, and was now emerging into the fresh air.

I came to realise over those first thirty days that in my endless wardrobe overhauls – which once seemed like a radical, final solution, but had over the years only increased in frequency, ruthlessness and desperation – and futile quest for a 'signature style', I was hunting for a lifestyle category I could just purchase

and slot neatly into: goth, geek, hippie, minimalist, 'quirky' girl...
I wanted the safety of a set of rules, limits for how I should dress,
look, live, think. I wanted to be 2D, a fictional character, able to
be summed up top-to-toe in a pithy descriptive paragraph. Neat,
tidy, unchanging, complete.

Through this challenge, I finally had to accept that there
is no point at which I will be 'finished'. It's not the nature of
human beings to be static. I will always be a work in progress
– changeable, chaotic, paradoxical, a cacophony of tastes and
desires and ideas and opinions. It is very freeing to accept this
as fact.

I will never 'finish' my wardrobe. There is not one true
hairstyle out there waiting for me to discover it. I will probably
never have a signature scent.

Nobody's tastes fit neatly into one style or subculture or
definition. Everyone has 'guilty pleasures' that don't fit with the
image they have painstakingly created for themselves. But why?
We are not meant to be 2D creatures. We can accept and like the
things that don't fit, the things that are opposites. The concept of
a 'personal brand' does us a disservice – it allows little room for
paradox, change or nuance, which are all essential parts of the
complexity that is human experience.

Unable to soothe this burgeoning cognitive dissonance in the
normal way, it slowly dawned on me that what I really wanted
was to break out of the cycle of being a consumer. I wanted my
wardrobe to consume less of my thoughts. I certainly never
wanted to experience the 'trance of greed' again.

Throughout May that year I tried not to overthink what I was
wearing, to be present in the moment, to notice how things
made me feel. I tried to work through my wardrobe and wear
everything – to see what fitted, what was comfortable, what I
still liked. I tried to read for pleasure, not simply to tick books
off my to-read list. And I tried to emphasise self-care, the

idea being that feeling good about myself could come from something other than my looks, my clothing. I realised I barely knew how to pamper myself any more – I'd been so focused on my appearance for so long that sitting in the garden with a cup of tea (as opposed to painting my nails, applying a face mask, or any of the other beauty treatments marketed to women as relaxing) was a revelation. When did female leisure time come to revolve purely around making oneself more attractive?

Emotionally, I rollercoasted all month between empowered and deprived. I struggled to define myself as a person in any way other than how I looked and dressed, but I noticed that I was becoming more interested in the world around me – in nature, history, travel, folklore, philosophy – things that had fascinated me as a child but simply become of less importance than my appearance as I got older. My previous steady diet of women's magazines, fashion blogs and influencers' feeds had been limiting, designed to keep the focus firmly on the self and its flaws (which, with enough time and money, you could fix, of course).

I found myself chasing memories of my childhood, as though I could tap into pure, unadulterated me by going back far enough. I sorted through old photos and paid a visit to the village where I grew up, but there seemed a vast gulf between who I was and who I had become.

By the end of the month I felt more purposeful and positive. I was enjoying keeping a journal, and I liked the sense of control over an aspect of my life, the realisation that I didn't have to be a slave to my impulses after all. The knowledge that I didn't lose anything by not buying something, that having or not having an item didn't change me as a person, had freed me from the spending trigger of trying to affirm my identity to myself, and not a moment too soon.

Chapter 2

The Comparison Trap

When I was pregnant with my little boy, I went to Wales with my partner and his father – two large, affable, mischievous Welshmen. It was a real, proper holiday, the kind I hadn't known I needed until I found myself in the middle of it, breathing a sigh of relief.

We had no Wi-Fi. No phone reception. I found myself, for the first time in eighteen years (give or take), cut adrift from the internet. And this turned out to be a bigger deal than I had expected.

This holiday was to a location where Dai and his dad regularly liked to go, plus or minus a motley assortment of brothers, sisters, nephews and dogs. It was not, therefore, selected via TripAdvisor. I had not spent evenings browsing Canopy and Stars for a location with maximum Instagrammability.[5] It was a place where I could feel things, do things, think things, but not share them. It was a place of realness, of being – ironically – connected.

Since childhood, I have felt driven to document my existence. As if, if I didn't present the sum total of my life and experiences for others to review, to admire, to pass judgement on, I didn't really exist. Therefore, to find myself under the warm summer sun with nothing but a good book and good company – and no way of telling people about it – I at first felt anxious, panicky. What use was a holiday if no one knew what a good time I was having? Every trip I'd taken since the advent of home internet had been dissected online, sometimes for a wide audience during my stint as a goth blogger. My trip to Cornwall several months previous had been photographed from every angle, and at the end of each day I stretched out my legs on the floral duvet of our B&B bed and presented that day's doings to Facebook, Instagram and Snapchat. As though that had been the point.

Part of the reason I stopped blogging was because I had started living my life *for* the blog – choosing my activities, experiences and outfits through the lens of how I would write it up later, and what I thought would look good to my readers. My every movement, choice, purchase was curated for my invisible audience. Instead of being me, I was performing me.

And now, a decade later, I hadn't stopped. My image had changed, my platform had changed, but the actions were the same. Haul posts. Selfies. Outfit of the day. Instagram was my favourite platform. I posted daily. My phone was connected to me by an invisible umbilical. Once outdoorsy, I could no longer function without Wi-Fi.

Worryingly, I noticed my attention span being obliterated – I stopped being able to read books without checking my phone every few paragraphs, then lengthy articles. I struggled to take in the meaning of the words on the page, I was so preoccupied. Soon I couldn't follow the plot of a movie because my attention was on my phone. My writing, a constant since childhood, dried up. In my teens, when we still had dial up and a PC, I'd often been online up to eight hours a day. Now, I was waking up at 2am to check for new likes.

At first, Instagram recaptured my childhood joy in documenting my world. From mixtapes to diaries, I have always enjoyed the process of capturing and showcasing snapshots of a given moment in time. I used the app like a photo diary, but four years in, clocking up around five hours of Instagram usage a day, I was not only addicted but concerned about the messages I was putting out. *Look what I've bought! Look how quirky I am! Notice me, you guys, I'm being authentic as hard as I can!*

Technology and shopping became irresistibly intertwined. Like an influencer? Buy her outfit. Toilet break? ASOS awaits. I didn't realise that what I was doing, essentially, was continually marketing to myself. I couldn't stop shopping until I stopped browsing. And when I tried to stop browsing... I couldn't.

Everything we do is online. For a long time, I thought that the best way to be myself in a world where everyone is watching was to strive for total transparency in the name of authenticity. I figured it was kind of punk rock to post bedheaded, no-make-up selfies, to not (appear to) worry about whether or not I looked good.

However, I wasn't *doing* anything in real life. Life was something that happened around me, outside the bubble I was in. Just as I once did with my goth blog, I was buying things and going places purely to have the photo to post online. Case in point: I recently looked back at some photos my friend Alice took when we had a girls' weekend in London. In all but one candid snap of me, guess what I'm doing? That's right, I'm on Instagram. Head down, looking at my phone. Even in the National Gallery, for goodness' sake.

I was addicted to Instagram just as I had once obsessed over my blog, to the detriment of all else. Except modern apps made the addictive, obsessive behaviours even more damaging – not only was I once again pouring all my time into an online persona, but this time the nature of social media meant that it was affecting my confidence, my sleep, my memory, my ability to converse, my manners... I was scrolling through Instagram during conversations, under the table. I knew it was pretty rude and obnoxious, but I could justify it by telling myself that other people did the same thing.

Escaping from my need to present my life, my thoughts, my heart and soul online, was difficult. Each day with my baby boy, I yearned to post each new expression, discovery and sound. He quickly learned to hate my phone as a rival, this thing that absorbed my attention and came between his eyes and mine, to the extent that he began to cry each time I reached for it.

When I started the shopping ban and was forced to cut down on browsing time, I remembered that trip to Wales and how pleasant life could be when I stopped being under the thumb of social media. Life for living, not a continual performance.

June came hot and humid. I'd deleted my social media apps and found myself abruptly adrift in reality, without the crutches I had become accustomed to. I started sleeping with my phone outside the bedroom, turned off notifications for email, and used my tablet only for reading ebooks. At first, I was irritable, anxious, checking phantom vibrations and hiding my phone in ever more tricky-to-access places to stop me picking it up habitually. I installed a timer app to keep my usage under control.

Unable to shop, unable to kill hours on social media, I found myself suddenly in possession of swathes of time. My son was no longer a needy loud creature distracting me from the important things I needed to do online, he was a little person, desperate for his mummy's undivided attention. I started baking cookies. I invited friends over. I started to go outside, taking the Spud for daily walks in the buggy.

Unfortunately, this newfound reengagement with the physical world proved to be my downfall, albeit in a very minor way. On Day 35 of the shopping ban, my dad took me and the Spud to a village fete. It was idyllic, quintessentially British; a blue sky with fluffy white clouds, thatched cottages, bunting riffling in the warm breeze. The Spud and I shared a bowl of fat ripe strawberries and cream in the shade of a mammoth oak tree. And, entirely without thinking, I got chatting to a local beekeeper selling her wares, and cheerfully, unthinkingly, broke the shopping ban – a £1 honey lip balm!

I didn't even realise what I'd done until we were in the car on the way home, and then I had to laugh – of all the things I could have bought, it certainly could have been worse. At least I'd supported a local craftsperson with my slip, and I was hardly the last of the big spenders! Still, I was a little disappointed at breaking my streak, and astonished at how mindlessly I had made a purchase.

Small mistakes aside, it was during this month that the reality of my financial situation began to sink in. With no further income of my own, the years ahead looked bleak and frightening. I started looking at our household budget to see what could be tightened up, the beginnings of an interest in frugality and thrift, a mindset which both my parents had tried to instill.

In an odd way, I felt sad at times at the prospect of going for such a long period without just buying whatever I wanted. But I could already sense that it might come to be liberating; more money for travelling, meals out, days at the beach, and freedom from indoctrination – perhaps I might develop an immunity to advertising, social media envy, comparison. How good might it feel, to just step off the consumer carousel and walk away?

It was around this time that I first watched a documentary called *The True Cost*,[6] which shows the damage caused to people and planet by Western society's addiction to cheap, fast fashion. (If you haven't watched it, I'd certainly recommend it.) In silence as the credits rolled, I felt the weight of all the clothes I had bought and never worn and given to charity shops, the impulse buys, the shopping sprees, the sale 'bargains', the piles of clothes on my bedroom floor, trampled and unappreciated.

For so many years I had bought unthinkingly, never stopping to consider where my clothes had come from, whose hands had cut the cloth and stitched the seams. I knew about sweatshops, of course, we all do – it's an uncomfortable truth we dance around and ignore as we pile clothes into our baskets in Zara and H&M. We are proud of our bargains. We think we are savvy shoppers. Meanwhile workers labour for a pittance in unsafe buildings and are gunned down in the streets protesting for fair pay.[7]

My concerns about being the worst-dressed in my friend

group, the problem of having too many clothes, seemed suddenly unutterably first-world and shallow. My shopping ban took on new meaning as I realised that my greed and wastefulness were contributing to this horrific state of affairs. In the face of Rana Plaza and the thousands of garment workers who died when the building collapsed,[8] I sat mute, shocked and guilty. How could we be doing this to each other? In the name of *fashion*?! It was madness, that people were injured, dying, rivers poisoned, children enslaved, so that we in the West could continue to buy – and thoughtlessly, relentlessly dispose of – more cheap clothes and fleeting trends than we know what to do with.

For a long time I had avoided looking at myself and my habits, at the impact of my actions. Now I had stopped avoiding the facts, I couldn't put my head back in the sand. It's too easy to gloss over where things come from, and although I'm only one person and I knew my shopping habits alone wouldn't change the world, I also knew I didn't want to be part of the problem and keep contributing during my lifetime to such a harmful industry.

My plan going forward – after the shopping ban – had been to try to save money by buying clothes more cheaply. Now I didn't think I could buy a brand new £12.99 dress without wondering which individual, less fortunate than myself, would be carrying the real cost. Yes, I needed to save money, but perhaps the best way to do that was to just not buy so damn much and to start taking better care of what I already had.

By July '19, two months into my shopping ban, I was becoming irritated by my inability to stop thinking about clothes. On days out, I found myself constantly playing the comparison game against other women, and I'd noticed the snarky voice of my inner critic carping at me: "Your shoes are wrong, you haven't got the figure for that, who do you think you're kidding?"

When friends visited, I felt sloppy, awkward and underdressed.

If I put on make-up and made more effort with my outfits, I felt overdone and vapid. Whatever I did, I perceived myself as somehow wrong and out of place. I felt deflated every time I saw someone with what I perceived to be a better ensemble, and became envious of women who didn't seem to care what they wore and were still at ease with themselves. I was getting increasingly frustrated, and wanted to just forget about how I looked. When had my appearance taken over my life to this extent? It was as though the disordered eating behaviours I had overcome had simply been replaced by other damaging behaviours. I had read so much about body acceptance and self-love, but I had to face the facts – if I really loved myself, I wouldn't be spending my hard-earned money to fix imaginary problems, or constantly comparing myself to strangers.

Comparison was an extremely difficult habit to escape. There was a point when I thought I might never free myself from it, and was doomed to spend the rest of my life measuring myself against every woman (or anyone at all with an outfit I particularly liked) that I encountered, and finding myself lacking. It took almost a year of avoiding fashion content, particularly on social media, and trying to notice and disrupt my negative thought patterns before I suddenly noticed that the urge to compare had just... fallen away. I cannot overstate how liberating this felt.

Happily, a couple of months in, I was beginning to really enjoy the shopping ban. The stress and anxiety I had felt back in May were replaced by a newfound pleasure and satisfaction in removing myself from the consumer rat race. I had taken myself away from a source of guilt, envy, frustration and confusion, and I was achieving a simple joy from using what I already had.

It was frightening to think what I could have spent in the two-and-a-half months since starting the ban if I had continued unchecked. Worse, there was nothing at all I really needed, so I would have just found things I quite liked and convinced myself that they were necessities. It's amazing how brainwashed we are into consuming as a way of life, and it was a relief to take a step back and look critically at the mechanisms at work.

One benefit of giving up shopping that I noted at this time was that, as a direct side effect of giving up the preoccupation with my appearance that constant shopping had contributed to, I found my range of interests expanding. I was more likely – and able – to pay attention to a passing whim (say, to plant vegetables, or learn to play pennywhistle), instead of reserving my time and attention for the constant tweaking of my physical appearance. I hadn't realised to what extent I was stifling any interests that didn't relate in one way or another to my personal presentation.

On one family day out, my partner, the Spud and I ended up in Burley, a small village in the New Forest which draws a substantial tourist crowd for its ties to Wicca and witchcraft, as the home of the famous witch Sybil Leek. Full of shops packed with incense, crystals, jewellery, witch figurines, spell components, hippie clothing and more, it's a lovely quirky place and has long been one of my favourite places to visit. I had many of the shops there mentally earmarked as 'shops I wouldn't be able to resist'.

And yet, I didn't find myself tempted by a single thing. In fact, the phrase 'New Age crap' drifted through my mind more than once. I wasn't getting caught up by the atmosphere, the vibe of the place. I just... wasn't buying it.

In some ways it was a little sad that the dazzle of the magic shops no longer had the power to instill such wonder, but at the end of the day, a shop is just a shop, whether it sells esoterica or groceries, and all else is glamour, an illusion designed to get you to part with some cash.

Don't get me wrong... I strongly, firmly, utterly believe in magic! In many ways, I am the perfect victim – sorry, target audience, for the peddlers of Unicorn's Breath scented candles, crystal yoni wands, ninety-seven varieties of the mass-produced 'Witches Brew' mug, and what-have-you. Yes, all right, I own at least one velvet gown and more tie dye than most people have admitted to since the seventies. I am all for having a little enchantment in your life. It adds a bit of sparkle – even meaningfulness – to the everyday. It fuels creativity. I just don't believe that you can *buy* magic.

Yes, there are shops in which you can buy ingredients for every spell and potion you can think of. Yes, I once had a heavy interest in Wicca and bulk-ordered candles, velvet altar cloths, pentacle jewellery, herbs and all kinds of other paraphernalia, but over time I realised, well, it's just not very magical to shop for the entirety of your spirituality. Not least in our modern era, when your healing crystals could have been sourced from an industrial mine using the labour of underage workers,[9] and your cleansing herbs threatening the potential survival of a species.[10] Nothing very enchanting about that.

That said, many – if not most – Pagan and witchcraft supply stores are small businesses, often stocking handmade items and providing valuable support for their local communities. I do believe they are well worth supporting, particularly in these troubled times – I'd much rather buy a book from my hometown's 'wellness and esoterica' shop than from Amazon, for example. But I try not to buy what I could make, or grow, and I do like to ask about where things are sourced from, and how they're made. I feel it's important to encourage demand for more sustainably sourced products, not another ten dozen plastic broomstick pens.

In July we also took our first holiday as a new family, to the Isle of Wight. In a rare moment of prescience, I had booked and paid for the short trip during the early months of my pregnancy, guessing correctly that by this stage of the game Dai and I would be tired, stressed and desperate for a change of scenery. I didn't expect that I would have blown my savings, although my reluctance to ever look at my bank statements should perhaps have clued me in.

Previously, holidays had given me yet more opportunities to splurge. First of all, a new holiday wardrobe – sandals, shoes, floaty floral dresses, a floppy straw hat that would be annoying as heck to wear and never see the light of day again. Then I would buy the equivalent of another new wardrobe whilst *on* holiday, not to mention all the books and souvenirs. At some point I'd stopped looking at holidays and day trips as breaks or adventures – they had just become an opportunity to do some more consumption in a different place. This had hit its peak some years previous when I went by train to Whitby Goth Weekend – I set out with one suitcase and came back with five.

This time, things would be different. Dai had suggested I set myself a £1 budget to buy what he called "a proper souvenir" like a pin badge or stick of rock, as would have been the case when we were kids. At first, I resisted this idea, but eventually I realised I was looking for a loophole which would allow me to go and buy a new hoodie or whatever from some overpriced surf brand.

As it turned out, I didn't even spend as much as a pound on myself. Though we stayed just moments away from Shanklin Old Town and all its gift shops, nothing caught my eye or piqued my interest for more than a moment.

It wasn't lost on me that the best day of the holiday involved no phones, cameras or even money – we took the Spud swimming for the first time, and by good luck and happenstance we had the pool all to ourselves that afternoon. I'll never forget the brilliance of his smile and his delighted squeals.

It was also a turning point for me, as I hadn't worn a swimsuit of any kind in public since I was about fifteen years old. My body image is something that, like many women, I have wrestled with, and I'd simply stopped going swimming over a decade ago so that I didn't have to reveal my human, imperfect body. Bad skin and disordered eating had left me convinced that I would end up the butt of every joke if I ventured into the water. But I did it, once at the hotel pool, once at the beach, and absolutely nothing happened. No one looked twice at me. What a relief it was to discover that no one cared! Another blow against that carping inner voice.

Chapter 3

Been There, Done That...

Reviewing my holiday photos from the Isle of Wight, I noticed that my bikini was not providing me quite as much coverage up top as I needed – one thing on the beach, another thing entirely in the family pool at the leisure centre. So I allowed myself a ban waiver to purchase a swimsuit, with the proviso that it be ethically sourced (*The True Cost* still vivid in my mind's eye).

I ordered a paisley swimsuit from vintage store Beyond Retro, and when it arrived, I could not have been happier with it. I think I appreciated it more because I bought it to fulfil a legitimate need, and because it was second-hand, I didn't need to go through the exhausting, irritating faff of browsing and comparing 9,000 options. And I somehow felt it was more 'me' than a generic piece from Primark or H&M.

If only that had been my only ban break for August '19. In hindsight, it's hard to pinpoint a single trigger. I remember that we went on our annual pilgrimage to beautiful Pembrokeshire, and the deep dismay I felt discovering that our cottage, once a place of retreat and renewal, now boasted Wi-Fi. I felt unable to ignore it, despite encouragement to do so from Dai and his dad, and found myself furtively scrolling through Pinterest in the bathroom.

On our day trips to local beauty spots and seaside villages, my tendency towards comparison went into overdrive. I watched other women constantly, my chest aching with jealousy. I hated my clothes again. I felt old, frumpy, fat. I started sneaking off to the loo and browsing ASOS, Office, H&M, looking for the next fix, the 'perfect' item that would pull together my magpie wardrobe. Deep down I knew that the only thing that needed pulling together was me. My compulsion to shop, my fixation on my appearance as all-important, soured my mood and cast a pall over time in an idyllic place with my son and fiancé.

Returning home, I couldn't shake off those feelings. One afternoon, watching a makeover show on Netflix, I found myself almost in tears as the stylist encouraged her victims to express themselves creatively with their clothing, an outlet that no longer seemed to serve me.

One o'clock the following morning I started shopping. It began with an £8 dress in the Beyond Retro sale.

Then an £18 Glossier lipstick.

Then four pairs of jeans from Topshop.

And just like that, I was off the wagon.

The next two weeks passed in a sickly blur.

A package from Zara. A package from H&M.

Guilt, frustration, confusion, anger, disappointment.

A package from Pull & Bear. A package from ASOS.

Pinterest, fashion blogs, perfect women, perfect lives.

Nights spent scrolling, trying to picture that item, this item, on me, in my life. Squelching concerns about waste, about ethics – I can't explain why it felt so urgent, so desperate, why I felt clothes had the power to fix whatever it was I felt I was sorely lacking. I could feel myself becoming more irritable by the day, distracted, distressed by this apparent inability to dress myself.

I decided I needed to jettison some of these clothes I supposedly hated so much, and perhaps – hopefully – some of these stifling emotions along with them. Before I knew it my wardrobe was rattling with empty hangers. I had achieved the minimalist dream, the capsule wardrobe.

Despite three house moves over the course of the previous year, and what I thought was a fairly comprehensive clear-out each time, I still had a pretty enormous wardrobe. I even applied the full Marie Kondo[11] treatment, piling up all the items from each category and sorting through them all (it took me over a fortnight to clear the book pile). But because I had still been continually, mindlessly shopping, I could still barely move for clothes.

After reading Cait Flanders's blog[12] and learning about her super-minimalist 28-item wardrobe, a desire for a Pinterest-friendly, effortlessly curated closet kicked into high gear, and I resolved to clear everything out of my wardrobe that was only so-so, and keep only the things I really loved. The metal jaws of the Salvation Army clothing bank closed with a creak and a bang on a bizarre variety of things: an alarming amount of expensive shoes that hurt my feet, a T-shirt from a metal gig in Birmingham I spent the next eighteen months wishing I had back, miniskirts that looked fine at 25 but suddenly mildly embarrassing at 27.

I expected the result to be an airy sense of weightlessness, an ease of getting dressed. Instead I felt bored. My wardrobe may have been streamlined, all my choices now flattering, but I missed the sense of possibility. My closet felt tired and colourless, and with a sinking heart, I realised that – once again – I had simply been wasteful. I wasn't Cait Flanders – when would I learn that I couldn't become myself by emulating other people?

My clear-out did at least prove to me that, in shopping my way to a new persona, I had been buying the wrong things. Most of what I donated was two-a-penny; meaningless; pieces bought to fill a generic 'this is what your wardrobe is missing' list – tailored black trousers, a classic beige trench coat. But those things weren't me at all.

One thing I was learning during the ban was how to tell what I actually liked – not what I thought I should wear, or what would improve me, or what I'd wear if I was a slightly different version of myself, or would have really loved five years ago. I must have read the advice to not buy anything you don't really love dozens and dozens of times, but it had never really sunk in – or else I was so overcome by the buying urge that 'really love' was no longer objective. I could convince myself that I 'really loved' pretty much anything, and come up with umpteen apparently sensible justifications for owning it, only to realise the truth of the matter once said item was hanging in the wardrobe emanating guilt and vague discomfort.

But now I really, genuinely had nothing to wear – and I couldn't shop. A dilemma, if ever there was one.

I was back where I had started. Stressed, anxious, and broke, I felt like I was treading water. I was crippled with tension headaches and short-tempered with my son. I had to find some air.

I turned back to my journal, flipped through the pages, and remembered the sense of possibility and hope I had felt when I started to look at things through the lens of frugality and learn about sustainability. I had touched the edge of a new way of living, where how I might present myself was the least important thing about me. Where creativity and self-expression did not rely on what I chose to buy but who I chose to be.

Slowly, I felt calmness returning. I pushed aside the endless questions and doubts about my appearance, the stream of comparisons and envy, and did my damnedest to focus on other things.

Day 100 of the shopping ban – or what would have been – came and went. I consoled myself with the thought that I would have spent an awful lot more over the last three months had I not been putting my heart and soul into my challenge. It had been a shock to me how quickly I fell back into 24/7 browsing, shopping, and thinking about shopping. And I was astonished by how crap it made me feel.

I stopped the clear-out. It was making me worried and uncomfortable, wishing I'd left well enough alone. I was concerned about the time, money and effort it would take to replace what I was bagging up. I felt I was going too far in my need to reach a clean slate.

Three months of hard work, trashed in a few days! There had to be better ways of spending my time.

Once I had some breathing space, it was time to tackle the new set of problems I had now made for myself, a matched pair. One: I had once again devastated my finances, and there was only one last lump sum of holiday pay on the horizon, at the end of the month. I was going to have to figure out how to stretch that money as far as it could possibly go.

Two: I had devastated my wardrobe. In the ruthlessness of my clear-out, I had left myself next to nothing for daily life. It was all very well and good that these two party dresses and this winter blouse sparked joy, but what was I going to wear now?!

The second problem, after all that frenzied buying and discarding, turned out to be the easiest to fix. I set myself a £20 budget to hit the charity shops and replenish my naked closet.

After the intensity and guilt of the previous fortnight, I was – finally – shopped out. I couldn't summon up the energy to browse every rail and compare every item to try to curate the perfect selection of items that 'felt like me'. I went to British Heart Foundation. I picked up every item in my approximate size from the £2 or less rail. I took them into the changing room, and I bought everything that fitted that I didn't hate.

It was far from being the perfect wardrobe, mismatched and full of oddities, but I was resolved, now, to stop giving the whole matter such goddamn importance. I was sick of repeating the same cycle and learning nothing. The whole experience had reminded me why I'd wanted to get off this ride in the first place. I'd felt totally out of control, and that frightened me.

For a short time I muddled through, doing an awful lot of laundry as my new 'minimalist' wardrobe endured the daily deluge of baby food, milk, puke, and other things the bevy of well-dressed online influencers smiling benignly at their ethically produced ceramic mugs apparently weren't dealing with.

Then one day I was having a cuppa with a good friend, Bel, when I mentioned I was low on clothing options. Bel winced, laughed and said, "Well, I've just had a clear-out. Let me bring you a bag of stuff over and see if there's anything you want." I was delighted – even more so when she returned with an enormous shopping bag of lovely things.

Word soon spread amongst my social circle. My mum, bless her, dug out from the depths of her cupboard a bag of things she'd been meaning to take to a charity shop, and kindly returned to me a warm coat I'd given her the previous winter because I thought it was unstylish. The designer replacement I'd bought did nothing to keep out the wind – not an issue in June, but a nightmare in January.

One friend, Alice, turned up with a bag of clothes and an expression of pity. I'm not sure if she thought I was a charity case or just a bit of an idiot. Bridesmaid Topaz turned up with six binbags (yes, six – "I'm not a shopaholic," she firmly announced. "This has all been sitting in my mum's house since I went to uni. I haven't even looked at it in years. Do what you like with it,") for me to take my pick from. I was left with a bulging wardrobe (again), a sense of gratitude and great relief, and a new insight into the content of my friends' closets. It seemed I wasn't the only one with a tendency to accumulate an untenable amount of stuff.

I realised that the thousands of options online had only given me a sense of panic, of needing to keep up, of not-enough-ness. I had actually stopped browsing charity shops, prior to the ban, because I had come to feel that to make the exact right clothing choices and stop buying things I didn't wear, I needed the option to filter by size, brand or colour. I was overwhelmed by choices. Want jeans? Dark wash, acid wash, stone wash, sandblast, boyfriend, slim boyfriend, girlfriend, mom jean, skinny jean, super skinny, high waist, low rise, ripped, raw, ankle grazing, bootcut, flared, skate jean, balloon jean, cocoon, embroidered, slim fit, cigarette, stretch, jegging, bleached, cargo, frayed, button front, straight leg, cropped, distressed, crop flare, cuffed

hem, pleated, pom-pom trim, patched, plastic knee windows[13]...
A smorgasbord of choices. (I did not make any of these up!)

And yet, I still couldn't seem to find exactly what I wanted –
trend-driven fashion brands produce en masse, and their target
market apparently wasn't a twenty-seven-year-old new mum
with a round belly and boobs that require scaffolding.

Conversely, these new clothes of mine had been chosen from
a very limited selection. But they brought colour, and variety,
and I felt happy to have them. I also felt silly for not having
thought of asking my friends and family for help sooner. Was I
so locked into the consumer mindset that I had forgotten about
community?

I had also now seen first-hand the sheer volume of clothes already
at large in the world. Women and their overstuffed wardrobes
are the butt of many a movie joke (*Confessions of a Shopaholic*,
anyone?), but seeing the stress, financial pressure and even debt
people I knew were experiencing, caused by overshopping, I
wasn't laughing.

Retail therapy is promoted to women as the cure for whatever
ails us. I have bought new clothes to cheer up, to wind down, to
reinvent myself, to affirm myself, to celebrate an achievement. It
had become the norm for me to buy a new outfit for any given
occasion or night out. When planning my wedding, I put 'new
dress for hen party' on my to do list without even thinking about
it. It literally did not occur to me to wear something I already
had. And I doubt that I'm alone in this. In fact, Metro reported in
2017 that one in six young people won't re-wear clothes they've
been photographed in on social media;[14] a survey of 2000 women
cited by the Daily Mail found that an item of clothing is worn,
on average, just seven times.[15] During my ban, Dai overheard
a Primark shop assistant telling her colleague that she replaces
her jeans every six months, as she feels after that they are "worn
out".

With a culture that places so much emphasis on our appearance on the one hand, and treats clothing as a disposable commodity on the other, it was no major surprise that all my friends' wardrobes were bursting at the seams.

Having worked in a charity shop, I had seen first-hand a small portion of the millions of garments that are donated each year – many unworn. The shop I worked in received such a high volume of donations that we occasionally had to turn goods away, because we simply didn't have the physical space to take in any more! Yet despite the best efforts of staff and volunteers, charity shops in the UK only sell around 10% of the clothing they are given.[16] The rest – damaged or soiled items, but also unsold items in good condition – is sold to 'rag traders', who generally ship it to third world countries, where much of it ends up in landfill.[17] The second-hand clothing industry is worth billions of pounds, but it is also saturated. Second hand western clothing is no longer a hot commodity; there is just too much of it.[18] We are producing, buying, and disposing of so much excess clothing that even the developing world cannot make use of it.

In September, with a full, if slightly bizarre wardrobe, and a tired heart, I turned my mind to the next quandary – how was I going to keep my financial ship afloat? The state of my bank account was horrific – I was now worse off than before I started the challenge.

Firstly and obviously, I made sure to return as many of my recent purchases as I could. I put a date in the diary for a clothing swap party with my friends. I didn't expect to have much to contribute, but it seemed like a nice non-spendy way to get together.

Dai and I looked at ways we could tighten up the family food budget. Instead of buying baby meals and 'ping meals', my former staples (I could barely boil an egg), I got a Jack Monroe budget cookbook from the library and started learning to make simple, healthy food that we could all eat together. Cooking was more pleasurable than I had anticipated, and soon became a new creative outlet, and I took up baking bread as well.

Once I'd started to see a difference, saving money became addictive. I breathed down Dai's neck as we trailed the aisles in Aldi, making sure we got the cheapest products per kilo. I switched our energy and internet providers for better deals and moved my savings to higher interest accounts. I even cancelled Netflix (on the understanding that we would reinstate it if there were to be a new season of Happy). Without a regular income I didn't want to invest in stocks and shares, so instead I started buying premium bonds. I started doing product testing and online surveys for a bit of extra money – it wasn't a fortune, but it was something I could provide for the family coffers whilst still being at home with the little one.

And it worked! The holiday pay came in, making my bank account healthy again – and it stayed. At last, I had turned myself into a responsible adult, able to live within my means.

Over the next few months, I used the money we saved to save more money – buying reusable cotton cloths for the kitchen and the baby's bum (no more kitchen towels or baby wipes), a safety razor and shaving brush (bye, Gilette), and period pants (don't even get me started on the price of tampons). Happily, these changes were also better for the environment, and I was pleased with my new, greener way of living.

That September I turned twenty-eight. I was finding my late twenties a very different animal than the carefree early twenties, before stretch marks, shortsightedness, the indignity of maternity bras and an onslaught of household bills. Not to mention the unwanted guest at every occasion, the furrow developing between my eyebrows.

I no longer wanted to wiggle round town in a slip of spandex from Boohoo – or at least when the thought did occur, it was tinged with nostalgia for that apparently-fleeting time when shiny fabric with rather daring cut-outs had actually looked quite good. Last time I'd put false eyelashes on, instead of alluring, I was forced to admit that I looked deranged.

Apart from a growing suspicion that motherhood combined with my natural tendency towards introversion was making me old before my time, I found I was enjoying different freedoms. No, I couldn't now drop everything for a weekend in London on a whim, but I also no longer wanted or needed to present myself as universally desirable, which freed up a lot of time and headspace. Other women were my allies, not my competition. Daily leg shaving and uncomfortable underwear made out of bits of string fell by the wayside, and I really didn't miss them.

So this birthday, I thought long and hard about what I wanted to do. What kind of things did I *really* enjoy? In this new shopping-free existence, my pleasures were simple – eating, reading, fresh air, looking at interesting stuff. So Dai and I elected to travel to a nearby town which was holding a flea market.

Somehow, at the time, it genuinely did not occur to me that shopping at a flea market was still shopping.

It was a beautiful day, the sky a cheerful blue over the higgledy-piggledy red roofs, the steam trains puffing industriously into the station of the historic market town. It was pretty and quaint, and we bought coffee and pastries as we wandered the stalls, captivated by doll parts on royal blue velvet and a cross-eyed taxidermy stoat. I bought three ribbons made from recycled silk and reclaimed sari fabric, thinking I could use them to customise, well, something. At some point. Definitely useful, anyway. And ethical! Supporting local businesses, too, I practically deserved a medal. (Please insert your own facepalm emoji here.)

I found September challenging in one notable way. Having broken the ban so very spectacularly in August, I was now having immense difficulty in reining in my shopping behaviours. Despite how much I wasn't enjoying it, every day I was back online, checking the new arrivals pages of my favourite stores, or – in a new twist – 'researching' ethical brands, to, um, "make sure that I could buy what I wanted in the future, but, you know, from better companies". I was trying to put myself in the path of temptation. Even though I couldn't really afford it, let alone justify it, I was searching for something so beautiful, so right, that surely no one would say I shouldn't buy it.

This was how I discovered The T-Shirt.

The T-Shirt was made by a small business in an English seaside town I had visited and loved many years ago. It was dyed with environmentally friendly dye and silk-screened by hand with the name of the town, and a quirky print of a trawlerman mending his nets with his trusty dog by his side. In classic British navy blue – flattering on me – and white.

Wow, I thought, *that's so me*.

But no. I was on a shopping ban. It was not to be. And yet... It's barely an exaggeration to say that for most of the month my every waking thought was about The T-Shirt. I discussed it, I journalled about it, frankly I obsessed about it. I knew that sticking to the ban would give me more long-term benefits than any T-shirt – I wouldn't be learning anything if I didn't try to stick it out – but every occasion gave me new opportunities to try to get around my own rules. I should never have been browsing T-shirts in the first place. I was setting myself up to fail.

Between that and the ribbons I felt like I was back at the beginning. *One more thing, and then I'll stop. One more thing... And just one more.*

So I started planning a holiday for Dai, the Spud and me. I picked a place I had always wanted to visit, but had written off as too difficult, too logistically complicated. I chose Shetland. It gave me something to aim for with my newfound frugality, and also something to focus on other than acquisition. I felt that it was time to have a good hard think about the kind of life I really wanted, because salivating over a T-shirt wasn't it.

I'd been shying away from doing that because it scared me. Change scared me. Goals scared me. But if I kept putting it off, my life would fly by in a whirlwind of shopping lists, everything worthwhile sidelined in case it was too difficult.

Oh, but I bought The T-Shirt.

Chapter 4

How Extinction Rebellion Stole Christmas

By October, I was starting to see how much I was in my own head, and how much of that related to acquisition or image. Turning it over all the time, what my style should be or represent, what I could buy to make it so, as if my personality and existence were a puzzle I could solve only by shopping.

When had *stuff* become of such importance to me? I was surprised, and ashamed, to realise that the acts of acquiring, storing, and searching for things to own had taken the starring role in my life story. I had no long-term goals, no big ideas for what I wanted to do with my short time on earth, but I knew that the plan had never been to become the custodian of the Me Museum.

In his book *All Consuming*,[19] Neal Lawson points out that previous generations of humanity defined themselves by what they produced, whereas we now define ourselves by what we own, what we buy. Was it any coincidence that as my Instagram use went up and my obsession with shopping skyrocketed, I lost interest in drawing, writing, making art in myriad small ways?

I was amazed by how much more I was beginning to enjoy and appreciate the things I already had. DVDs, books, colouring books, notebooks, yarn and needles, sketchbooks... I could entertain myself for years without needing to buy a single new thing.

This was also the first month when I noticed a marked decline in those feelings of comparison that had been plaguing me. Rather than fretting about my style (or fashion, the vapid, twittering cousin of personal style), I simply put on my clothes and had done with it. Every now and again my brain helpfully suggested that I could be sexier, happier or more fulfilled if I just bought a new outfit whenever I wanted. But mostly I'd just... stopped thinking about it. What I had was enough. I was enough. A brief pang of wanting, and the feeling would pass.

It was around this time that The T-Shirt arrived. My skin had flared up, thanks to a foundation that really didn't agree with me, and my hair badly needed a wash as I'd just learned the hard way that some shampoo bars don't work too well in hard water areas. Neither looking nor feeling my best, I pulled on The T-Shirt, this life-changing garment, this thing I'd built up in my head as the one last touch I needed to be complete...

And I was embarrassed to admit that when I looked in the mirror, there was a distinct sense of anticlimax. I still looked a bit crap and felt a bit deflated. I was just wearing a different shirt.

Just like everything else hanging in my wardrobe, the high The T-Shirt gave me couldn't last beyond the point of purchase. I had been a sucker for a killer tagline and a good photography campaign. But it was still just a T-shirt.

As Christmas approached in the first year of the shopping ban, my newfound frugality and burgeoning environmental awareness were twisting me in knots as I tried to think of ways to participate in this orgy of gift-giving without decimating my savings or trashing the planet more than I could help.

Not too long before, I'd heard some rumblings about this radical environmentalist group called Extinction Rebellion[20] who were protesting in London, bringing city streets to a standstill, arguing against Fashion Week, and otherwise generally making a nuisance of themselves. I was intrigued. All this passion, chaos and rage seemed to have boiled up very suddenly out of nowhere – what was going on?

I'd had vague positive feelings about Greenpeace for a long time, but by and large was convinced that all that environmental stuff was pretty radical and woo-woo, the province of earnest, slightly scary hemp-smelling people with hairy armpits. But XR was not only huge but encompassing all kinds of people – doctors and grandmothers, businessmen and schoolchildren. I was intrigued despite myself, and decided to look them up.

With my sleeping child in my arms, I watched an XR video entitled The Truth.[21] At first, I was just interested. Then I was shocked. Then I felt the bottom drop out of my stomach. As the girl with the punky haircut explained feedback loops and melting permafrost and food shortages and rising sea levels, I gripped my tablet in numb hands.

Does everyone know about this? Why isn't everyone panicking? What have we done? Oh, holy shit...

The full scale of the climate emergency caught me off guard and unsuspecting, a sucker punch to my sense of security and stability. I'm not ashamed to say, I wept. I'd brought a child into a world with a very uncertain future, and I felt powerless to protect him.

Let me loop back from existential dread to Christmas shopping (two things that go nicely hand in hand, I often find). After learning about the climate emergency, I found I had no more urge to buy joke presents, or anything really that people might not want or wouldn't use. The first year of the ban I was just a ball of stress – eco-anxiety plus wanting to find the best possible gifts plus money being a little tight equalled worry from October onwards.

Some of my friends arranged a Secret Santa using a wish list app. Enthusiastically, I filled my list with books, bath bombs and charity gifts – only to discover that the theme for the event was "dirty/inappropriate". I felt deeply humourless and a bit of a wally but just could not bring myself to buy a plastic penis of any description having just watched XR's video about, basically, the end being nigh (in the end I plumped for a book of howlingly bad self-published erotica and, okay, a penis-shaped lipstick. Apparently, there's a gap in the market for sustainable or zero-waste erotic gifts...). I kept picturing every hen party inflatable penis sticking up from landfill – outliving us. (Told you – humourless.)

For everyone else, I considered crafting gifts, and whilst this is something I've got more confident about, in 2019 I was still wrapped up (pun intended) in consumer culture and I was worried I would seem stingy or thoughtless.

Instead I decided I would support small local businesses. This turned out to be a bit of a bust – in my small town I only knew of a few local craftspeople, and I quickly discovered that doing my entire Christmas shop with them would leave me all but bankrupt. Eventually, cross and frustrated, I did my shopping exactly as I normally would, except I shopped in my hometown instead of travelling to a big city mall or market (and minus the 'one for you, one for me' mathematics I have been known to apply in years previous).

The following year, I must note, I was better prepared. I shopped mostly online (pandemic!), but I chose items from small businesses in the UK and favoured companies using sustainable materials and processes. It all sounds a bit 'worthy', I know, but I don't in good faith want to keep pouring my family's resources into environmental destruction. To me, it's been worth a little more thought and a little more time.

I also bit the bullet in the first year of the ban and had a chat with friends about setting a budget for our gifts, as in our mutual affection and enjoyment of gift-giving it was all getting a bit out of hand. One or two friends suggested that we no longer buy gifts for each other but focus on the littles instead. The rest of us agreed a £5 budget, which chafed at first but came to remind me of childhood Christmases, when we were given 'token' gifts (often practical or edible) which were given with great love but caused the giver little stress, financially or otherwise. I also have one friend with whom I tend to exchange secondhand books – it works for us.

I realised that my personal Christmases had been overshadowed by worry. I was overthinking it, competing against the imaginary Joneses and their perfect Christmas gifts, and it was leeching all the enjoyment out of the process.

All the time the shopping ban was ticking on in the background. Some days I questioned whether it was even really a good idea – wasn't life going to be dismal and ascetic without a little treat from time to time?

But my definition of 'treat' needed some tweaking. During the ban I'd bought a £1 honey lip balm – that was a treat. Not the expensive shoes and perfumes I was looking for excuses to buy. Treats could be free, too, I was remembering, or at the very least take up no space – the library, a mocha dusted with nutmeg, a bowl of fresh strawberries and cream, a box of macarons, a walk by the river, a cuppa accompanied by a good sunrise. I hadn't exactly been living a life of deprivation without the occasional shopping spree.

In fact I was starting to feel really grateful for all the things I now had, which before had been taken for granted, or which I'd planned to replace with 'something better'. I started reading 'frugal living' blogs, looking for ways to stretch our family budget. Suddenly I was implementing all sorts of new (to me) strategies to try to keep money in the bank – going a few more days between shampoos; going through the Spud's next-size-up clothing stockpile so I could fill the gaps cheaply rather than panic-buying when he needed something.

The Spud's wardrobe was largely second-hand anyway, which I sometimes felt a bit guilty about, but now I was grateful that the generosity of friends and neighbours had saved me the need to find, choose and buy hundreds of baby items. I would have spent considerably more, and because of the cost I would probably have felt the need to have everything coordinated, which really isn't necessary for such a young baby. In fact, with a sinking feeling I came to realise that in the first few months of the Spud's life I had wildly overspent on him.

It was easy to justify – *I only want the best for my child!* – but I could see that as a new mum, I had been floundering, and I had used numerous gifts and baby purchases to try to cover the fact that I didn't feel I was bonding with my son, I had no idea what I was doing, and frankly, I felt lost and terrified. Not to mention exhausted! The Spud breastfed round the clock, and there were nights I cried with sheer tiredness and thought about packing my bags.

New parenthood is rarely easy, despite the image so often perpetuated by social media yummy mummies. My birth experience had been – not to put too fine a point on it – a massacre, and the aftercare deeply lacking, so when I then found myself at home after a long, unexpected hospital stay with a newborn who wouldn't sleep unless he was held, and an impressive set of stitches, I felt nothing short of traumatised. For a while I became reclusive, and I was resentful – almost frightened – of this squeaking, squalling beetroot-faced tyrant in my arms.

Christmas approached when the Spud was two months old, and I still didn't feel as adoring as I thought I should. Terrified someone might notice I was a weird, ungrateful, abnormal mother, I ordered a great raft of luxury gifts for him from Harrods, Hamleys and Selfridges (paying extra for the branded gift boxes in case anyone missed the point). I think this was when the overshopping really kicked up a notch, as after Christmas I decided to revamp my wardrobe... You know the rest.

Suffice to say, my two-month-old bundle was not impressed by Selfridges, Steiff or anything else, although he quite liked the wrapping paper and the Christmas tree lights. I'd just used conspicuous consumption to hide my insecurity – it hadn't really been about the Spud at all.

Bonding was a long and arduous process – aided by Dai in

the early days, who made a show of the Spud "giving me a kiss" and "bringing me a coffee" every morning. My son's baffled blue eyes as he was lowered to my face for this 'kiss' never failed to make me giggle. (Nowadays he does give me a slightly violent kiss when the mood takes him, but he's more likely to put a Duplo brick in my coffee than make it for me.) But we got there, and there was nothing I could have bought, no amount I could have spent, that would have made those early days any easier. Giving another being round-the-clock care was more taxing than I had been braced for, and I felt the lack of autonomy very keenly.

As an introvert with many hobbies, I found it difficult to put a huge chunk of my inner life on hold. Only seeing how quickly the Spud grew made that any easier – soon I was able to see how fleeting all-consuming babyhood is, and realise that whilst he won't want me to cuddle him for hours forever, my books and crafts will still be there.

This wasn't the first time I'd learned to loosen my grip and take a more philosophical approach. By the time Dai and I got engaged, I had been living free from disordered eating behaviours for four years, and I believed that I was fairly comfortable in myself. Post-baby, my weight had gone up quite a bit (or at least, my dress size had – I don't own a set of scales), but I quite liked having a softer, curvier figure and I wasn't bothered by my stretch marks. Birth was the most incredible, awful, arduous thing I had ever undergone – it seemed only logical that it would leave a mark behind.

I thought I was pretty happy with myself and had avoided the traps and pitfalls laid by the industries who profit from getting women to feel badly about their appearance. However, the February before the shopping ban, I discovered that the beauty standards of the dominant culture can get in your head without you noticing, and smack you across the chops out of the

47

blue. For me, it was the day I tried on my wedding dress.

I'd taken a risk and ordered a dress online, from a designer on Etsy. I was so excited when it arrived, wrapped in layers of delicate tissue, pink and blue confetti hearts spilling out of the box as I lifted yards of tulle gently, reverently into my arms.

I'd thought it would take me months and months to find a dress. I wanted tulle. I wanted blush pink. I wanted a long train. I wanted buttons, not a corset-style lace-up back. And I found it the first day of looking. I'd never imagined myself in a strapless wedding dress, let alone a ballgown – too traditional – but on the model it looked like something from a fairytale. I remember catching my breath and thinking, I'd really feel like a *bride* in that dress.

But when I tried it on, I didn't feel like a bride at all. I felt like a frumpy troll. What an idiot I had been, to buy such a feminine dress, when I was such a great ugly lump. The wedding guests would fall about laughing.

I rang my mum in tears. "I hate the dress," I sobbed. "It'll have to go back." But I felt sick. If I didn't feel happy in a lovingly handmade fairytale gown that ticked all my boxes, what would it take?

Luckily for me (and my dress), my bridesmaids came swooping to the rescue. They stuffed me back into the dress and took photos while I laughed and smiled with them. When they showed me the pictures, the troll I'd seen in the mirror was gone. The laughing woman in the photos was radiant and joyful. She wasn't the slim blonde model from the website, she was me, with my bad skin and more teeth than a happy beaver, but I was glowing, and I looked great. The dress looked great on me, baby weight, henna-ed hair, tattoos and all.

I realised I'd been freaking out because I didn't look like an airbrushed model. I'd swallowed the wedding propaganda hook, line and sinker, and I'd beaten myself up because I didn't think I looked how a bride 'should look'. I was so disappointed that

I had nearly let poor self-image and stupid patriarchal beauty standards affect our big day, and surprised, too – recovered from disordered eating, I was usually pretty relaxed about my looks, and I was shocked by my own visceral reaction and the surge of shame and disgust I had felt.

The Great Dress Debacle was not the only occasion during wedding planning when I felt the pressure for things to be perfect, and I had to make it my mission to let go of impossible standards. As my experiences in motherhood and my mismatched wardrobe were fast teaching me, if you try to micromanage every detail, you're on the road to disappointment. Screw Pinterest weddings. I was going to aim for fun, memorable, and ending the day legally married to the man I loved. If there was something blue at my wedding, it damn sure wasn't going to be me.

So instead of panicking over everyone looking at me, I kept telling myself "they've all seen you before! They know what you look like!" and doing what would make me and Dai happy, whether it would look good on social media or not.

Don't get me wrong, I still had wobbles. I nearly had a meltdown at a wedding fayre wishing we could afford an events designer to make the reception hall into an enchanted forest (with white blossom trees on the tables, tea lights in glass globes hanging from their branches, and gold lace table cloths... It *was* beautiful, I admit), but there was just no way we could shoehorn it into the budget. Instead we planned our own decor for the cost of just one such arrangement, with dried flowers from a local florist, beer bottles we rather enjoyed sourcing ourselves, wooden rounds handmade by a friend working in woodland management, and little succulents in pots.

When you plan a wedding, you'll never please everyone. Assorted relatives offered 'helpful' criticism during the planning stages, and we had to learn to shrug it off and carry on regardless. I eventually came to realise that everyone's 'perfect' wedding would be different. This one was going to be chaotic, colourful, quirky, utterly imperfect (trying to coordinate wedding outfits whilst still breastfeeding multiple times a night led to little quirks such as the groom's buttonhole clashing with the bride's hair ornaments... All you can do then is own it like you did it on purpose) and *ours*.

I could have sweated over every detail. I could have bought matching floral robes for the bridesmaids for a single getting-ready photo. I could have hired a car for a grand entrance, got hair extensions, dieted into a smaller dress, fake tanned, mani-pedi-ed, Wonderbra-d, freaked out about every pimple and pore. Blown the budget on a candy floss machine and a temporary tattoo station and a photo booth and a doughnut wall and a personalised cocktail menu and vintage tea cups as favours... And it still could never be perfect, because there's rain and mud and breast milk, ill-timed farts and stray eyebrow hairs, and who the heck would I be trying to impress anyway? Strangers on the internet, or my friends and family who love me already and really wouldn't notice the lack of a rose gold balloon arch?

My friend Topaz noted in the bridesmaid group chat that I looked "like a majestic jellyfish queen" in my wedding dress. Indeed. And what more could any woman want?

As it turned out, I was grateful I chose to take the philosophical approach. Our wedding was planned for May 6th, 2020, when the coronavirus pandemic was newly devastating the country. We postponed twice and eventually had to cancel – all I could do was continue trying not to get my knickers in a twist over things that were out of my control.

Chapter 5

Lockdown

The start of the first UK lockdown affected me very strangely. In the house all day with a lively toddler – except for our daily walk around the nature reserve, which I think kept us both sane – I suddenly felt sick of all the stuff we had around us. I started scrutinising everything in our home with an eagle eye. This throw may have been perfectly acceptable and useful as a lap blanket, but did it really bring me joy? Did it? *Did it?!*

Every day Dai came home from work to find that more of our belongings had migrated to the cupboard under the stairs. But a few days later, I'd get weepy and emotional and put everything back. Then, waking up in the morning, I'd find my books and ornaments suddenly intolerable, and the whole thing would start again. I had to run out of the house in my sock feet early one day to retrieve some irreplaceable sentimental items from the recycling before the bin men arrived. This declutter/reclutter cycle, with its accompanying emotional highs and lows, went on for more than a month.

I realised that there must be something about minimalism that kept me coming back, even when one failed declutter after another seemed to be saying that this lifestyle wasn't for me. It was true that the spartan aesthetic so often associated with minimalism didn't capture my imagination. Besides, we'd experienced that form of sparse, modern, neutral style in our council estate house for the first few weeks after we moved in, and the effect was grim. Like living in a beige shoebox.

After bagging up my CDs, childhood toys, Tarot cards, excess clothing and art supplies – and then putting them back again – for what I hoped would be the final time, I realised that a different approach was needed. I had no problem parting with

DVDs we hadn't enjoyed or passing on clothes that didn't fit any more, but my new awareness of the environmental crisis that our excess consumption was creating meant I really didn't like being wasteful. If I could use something, I wanted to use it.

I was also forced to admit that I didn't want to get rid of sentimental items. I had pared down my photos and let go of those things I no longer felt any attachment to, but just as I didn't want bare walls and a Spartan home, I also didn't want to get rid of all my childhood toys or gifts from loved ones. When I realised this, I unboxed my oldest toys and arranged them on top of my wardrobe where I could see them and enjoy them. These were not 'clutter', these were things I treasured, and trying to force myself to get rid of them was only causing me stress and upset.

I had to trust myself to recognise what really was extraneous. And I didn't want to just swamp the charity shops with my castoffs, either. I began approaching my unwanted items with a 'rehoming' mindset – would a friend like this book? Would my mum wear this jumper? Could I sell this doll on eBay (and get some extra money into the bargain)? Yes, it took longer, but I felt that taking this time and effort was a step in the direction of taking responsibility for my consumer excess. It was instilling the lesson of caring for my belongings – of not participating in a throwaway culture – in a way that a big declutter and a trip to the Salvation Army never had.

So why did I keep coming back to the concept of minimalism? Clearly, I was never going to own less than 100 items (or whatever), and I was no longer invested in decluttering in favour of using, wearing out or rehoming.

Marie Kondo suggests that we start by forming a vision of the kind of life we want. Well, I had tried and tried, and frankly had no idea. Pinterest boards only made me more confused. Apparently, I liked most things – a cluttered bookshelf here, a folksy narrow boat there, a country cottage decked in florals, a sleek Copenhagen apartment. Once again, I had to look beyond the stuff. What was the appeal of these images? They told me I valued a pleasant home, simple joys, a sense of freedom, creativity and self-expression.

That was a start. I could see then that I kept coming back to those minimalist bloggers and writers because their work provoked a sense of expansiveness, of prioritising something more than things.

Then I knew what my next step was. My shopping ban was still the most important part of my plan – a pause in the influx of new things, a breathing space. Next, I too had to start prioritising something other than things. Decluttering had seemed like the answer, but it was still a focus on *stuff*.

I knew that writing regularly, a habit I had long neglected, could begin to fulfil the need for creativity and expression. But what about that freedom and expansiveness? How could I get some of that without buying things *or* throwing them away? I thought about the minimalist books and blogs I had read, and I decided that next I would focus on my health. I hadn't really exercised in years. Perhaps a regular yoga practise could bring a feeling of expansiveness to my physical body? I started rolling out my mat on the patio in the mornings, although my son did like to drive his lorries underneath me or sit on my head. And perhaps walking in nature, or learning a new craft, or finally picking up my guitar again, would give me freedom?

Slowly I stopped wanting to get rid of everything my eyes rested on. I taught myself to spin yarn (I had a drop spindle and some wool roving kicking around that I bought on impulse at a Christmas market), and to darn. I grew my first crop of vegetables in our garden. Between keeping my hands and mind busy, and actually using the things I had been keeping hidden away in the cupboards, I soothed my agitated lockdown brain and was able to create instead of consume.

May 2020 marked the end of my first attempted shopping ban.

Frankly I was surprised I'd remained interested and motivated for a whole year. I hadn't even particularly realised, until I started reading back through my journals, how my life had started to change since I quit overshopping.

On sunny afternoons that summer, we went foraging, and we ended up with so much homemade elderflower cordial that we were able to distribute bottles amongst family and friends. I was becoming aware of a new contentment, a peace of mind that I could never have purchased. I felt more connected to my loved ones – gift-giving had become a source of pleasure and joy rather than stress – and my enjoyment of nature and the outdoors was reaching new heights.

As the lockdown restrictions eased, my mum emailed me a special offer from Travelodge – budget prices from July, so I booked three days in the village of Glastonbury, one of my favourite places, for me, Dai and the Spud.

Towards the end of June, through my work with Greenpeace – I had started volunteering for Greenpeace the previous November, as I was so shaken by Extinction Rebellion's video explaining the truth about the climate crisis that I felt desperate to do *something* – I ended up taking part in the Climate Coalition's The Time Is Now mass virtual lobby, for which I had to take part in a Zoom meeting with my MP. I'd actually initially chickened out of setting up a meeting but then decided I'd better walk my talk. I made a page of notes from Greenpeace's briefing and asks, and I was very glad that I had, because in the event, of the twenty people in my constituency who had signed up to attend, no one appeared but me! (One other lady tuned in twenty minutes late; I have never been so glad for the presence of a stranger.)

It was absolutely terrifying. I was shaking, and my voice went really high-pitched, but I delivered the list of asks and managed to mention some quite frightening statistics I had learned about how nature-deprived the UK is compared to the rest of Europe, and the sorry state of our tree cover, and also how lifeless and meek the government seems to be with regards to the climate emergency. The Climate Coalition host sent an email afterwards saying that I and the other lady had done "incredibly", and that ours was the only meeting where only one person turned up at the start (great...). I was really proud of myself, and glad I'd done it.

In July, the evil tag team of Instagram, eco-anxiety and shopping addiction came barrelling into my life. I'd set up an Instagram account to document my no-buy year – I hoped it would keep me accountable, and it obviously seemed like a good idea at the time.

It wasn't.

Inspired by my new online community of eco-friends (their word, not mine!) I started trying to radically overhaul our life. Now, I do think that cloth nappies, organic veg boxes, natural cosmetics, growing vegetables, foraging, composting, crafting, bamboo toilet paper, home baking, charcoal water filters, toy libraries, visible mending, natural dyes, bee saver kits and so forth are all good things... However, trying to invest in and do all of these things in the space of a single month exploded my budget and didn't do my peace of mind many favours either. I was also spending a couple of hours each day on Instagram, which brought my mood down without fail. Everything I was doing still didn't feel like *enough*. At first, I enjoyed being part of an eco-community, but after a while, every time I picked up my phone, I felt like I was being bludgeoned with more things I *ought* to be doing.

I found it slightly alarming at times that I'd suddenly become this person who cooks and darns things and grows vegetables and gets excited about birds. Adding the pressure to promote my new lifestyle on social media and also change the world by buying everything marketed as 'sustainable' was overdoing it.

Yes, I was extremely worried – terrified, actually – about the climate. But sustainability isn't simply something you buy, and blowing my recently restored savings wasn't going to save the human race all by itself (sadly). I do believe in supporting the supply chains that try to do good things and mitigate the bad, but I also believe in buying less. And I didn't want to undo the positive changes in my own life that had been wrought simply by taking control of my shopping.

So I got Dai to change my Instagram password, and deleted the app. I tried to go easy on myself – I didn't screw up the environment by myself, and I can't magically fix it either.

I wanted to stay anchored in the world around me, the world that over the last few months had filled up with colour, as if I was coming back to life instead of just getting out of my own head.

Our trip to Glastonbury rolled around, shortly before my birthday. As usually happens when I find myself in places where everyone is a bit alternative in manner of dress, I felt a bit boring and basic. Sometimes I feel I can't win with this. If I bust out the velvet dresses and shitkicking boots I feel self-conscious and like The Weird Friend™. If I wear jeans and T-shirt, I feel plain and unimaginative. But the comparison is a far cry from what it used to be, and I don't need dreadlocks and a cupboard full of dubiously sourced crystals to be interested in the environment or to enjoy Glastonbury.

We had a busy weekend of sightseeing, drinking blackberry mead in our hotel room and (in my case) looking hopefully for faeries, and I had no difficulty with refraining from shopping until the very last day, when I broke on all counts. I couldn't resist an Instagram post, and I bought three items of clothing. I was disappointed with the first point, but not the second in the end. Although I was time-pressured (Dai and the Spud were waiting in the car) and budget-constrained, the three pieces I bought – essentially on impulse, wanting to capture the sense of excitement, unconventionality and free-spiritedness I was feeling – have turned out to be three of the most-worn, most-loved and useful things I own!

Before I decided I was going to make some purchases, shopping ban be damned, the Spud and Dai and I sat eating our breakfast and drinking our much-needed coffee at a spindly table in the village square, basking in the sunshine. I was hunched over my phone, researching the ethical credentials of the shops I planned to visit, until I was satisfied I could give myself the green light to go ahead without guilt on that front. (Some people might have walked into the shops and talked to people, asked questions of the staff. I was not feeling bold enough that day!)

Coming home from Glastonbury I felt quite rejuvenated. I expect that, living in a place that is largely pretty conservative, it's healthy to be reminded that it's okay to be a bit more 'out there'. A lot of my wardrobe felt a little lacklustre in comparison to my new things. I had been playing it safe for a long time – worried about attention, or vanity, or consumerism. I'd almost forgotten the joy of impulse-buying something that is exactly right, or choosing a book in a real, physical bookshop. Non-chain-store shopping that is ethical and vibrant and brings a little excitement. Surely this was not the same animal as the blind, semi-desperate basket-filling I used to do in Primark, IKEA, Zara, it's-cheap-so-I'll-have-it? Was it selling out to consumer culture to take joy in well-chosen material objects, to appreciate the things we use and cherish them, not buy them to be used once and discarded?

Browsing online started to frustrate and irritate me. I couldn't find items that produced the same spark, especially since I wasn't sure what keywords to use or where to look. Standard labels we use like 'hippie' or 'alternative clothing' mainly turned up stuff that was mass-produced, sweatshop-made and unoriginal, which wasn't at all what I was looking for (is it 'alternative' if you bought it from the same website or brand that all the other 'alternative' kids are shopping from this week? What's unique about what amounts to a goth-in-a-box kit from Attitude Clothing? Tell me how that's less basic than buying all your clothes from New Look).

On my birthday, I decided that the shopping ban was to be no more. I wrote in my journal, "I want to be able to treat myself without guilt – enjoy books, films, music and art as and when I want to without feeling bad about it. And I want to learn to find a balance between spending and being frugal without going to one extreme or the other."

Except... not so much. Online browsing, annoying and unsatisfying though it was, quickly filled up my spare moments. Within three days I'd bought six clothing items, an art piece, and some more books. Whilst the items were great, I knew I couldn't afford for this to continue. So I reinstated my limits.

I wanted to enjoy my clothes, but I didn't want to go back to having to prove how 'alternative' I was by buying into a 'look'. And I didn't want to spend hours online, fruitlessly searching for – what, exactly? I felt like an exciting, enchanted, magical life was out there, but I just didn't know how to find it or create it. I had deduced, however, that it was not for sale on Etsy.

Chapter 6

Authenticity

Now that I'm actually, finally getting a handle on my shopping habit, it seems only fair to share those things that help. What works for me personally is that I have built these ideas into my life as habits, and over time they have worn away the sharp poky edges of my desperate wants and desires, so I don't feel that nagging urge to buy, buy, buy in the back of my brain, like an itchy label.

Simply put, I've learned better ways of dealing with at least some of the underlying unmet needs – a brief selection: insecurity and lack of self-esteem, need for approval, self-expression, need to be recognised as an amazing limited-edition snowflake with excellent taste in music, desire for a sense of belonging – which were fuelling my overshopping habit.[22]

My biggest weapon against overshopping is spending time outdoors. As the Spud has gotten older, we've increased the amount of time we spend outside from a begrudging half hour walk with the pram to as much as six hours walking around and playing at the park, and a minimum of an hour, rain or shine. In lockdown we took a daily walk around our local nature reserve and spent time tending our herbs and vegetables in the garden.

I don't always feel like dragging myself outside, but the Spud is insistent, and it makes me feel better about plonking him in front of Tractor Ted while I take a breather from time to time. And once I get out there, even if it's grey, mizzling and blowing a gale, after half an hour or so I generally morph into Annoying Nature Lady, getting excited about fluffy moss and interesting lichen.

One thing I know is that the more time I spend outdoors – preferably in nature, but a trek to the post office will do in a pinch

– the calmer and more content I feel. I usually leave my phone at home too, which frustrates some of my relatives but does me the world of good. It was initially a wrench to go out gadgetless, but in the year or so I've been going phoneless nothing dire has happened and everyone has largely gotten used to the fact I'll get back to them when I'm ready.

For best results, as my two-year-old has taught me, you need to actually interact with the nature – squelch in the mud, paddle in the river, listen to the birdsong. Mooching about with your eyes on Facebook and your headphones in won't actually do you any good. Also, don't forget to bring snacks. I have learned to always take along a peanut butter sandwich as we're always out longer than I expect!

This has evolved into a newfound love of the outdoors, and is probably the most I've spent time outside since I was a child myself. I've got tan lines on my feet, my complexion is about as good as it's ever been, and I feel better in myself, physically and mentally. I realise not everyone has the ability to access nature as we are lucky enough to do; fresh air, natural light, a view of the sunset and a bit of birdsong go a long way. I think the reason this helps is that it reminds me I'm one tiny part of a huge and intricate web – it really puts my worries about clothes and make-up and whatever into perspective. It also reminds me how incredible everything is. You don't get that sense of awe and wonder in TK Maxx.

Inspired by books such as *Timeless Simplicity*,[23] *Radical Homemakers*[24] and *Big Magic*,[25] I eventually realised that creativity isn't just about being an Artist (Capital-A) or a Writer (Capital-W) but is a way of living. It's a way of living that in particular is directly antithetical to constant consumption, as the rigours and stimulation of overshopping and excessive screen time seem to wither imagination – and happily, vice versa.

Living a creative life will mean something different to every person, but it requires time, care and attention. It could be home cooking, growing veg, painting, acting, figure skating, quilting, dance, playing the trombone, zine making, fashion design, keeping a beautiful home, soapmaking... All the unnecessary but fulfilling ways that humans have made ordinary life into something beautiful and satisfying.

I know a person who does creative things all the time but describes herself as "not creative". Yet this lady puts together beautiful outfits and colourful make-up looks every day, writes poems, and once presented me with a stunning hand-painted glass bowl. She also raised children, which takes a *lot* of creativity. We have developed some strange ideas about what creativity actually is, and there are probably a lot of people shutting themselves off from various forms of self-expression because someone told them they weren't artistic, or talented, or 'being realistic', or were wasting time.

It doesn't have to be complicated and you don't have to try to make a living from it. Over the last couple of years I have tried my hand at knitting, crochet, cooking, baking, singing (purely for pleasure, as I am tuneless), jive dancing, playing guitar and pennywhistle, and making my own house cleaning and beauty products. I want to fill my life with the richness of doing, even if I'm not very good at everything I turn my hand to, rather than spending my days passively consuming what other people have made.

I did eventually realise that my frantic brand of decluttering had cleared my physical space but done nothing for my state of mind. It was time to make a serious effort to slow down and stop rushing from one task to another. I had been spurred on by the high I get from clearing stuff out, to the extent that I was often up at night, racking my brains to see what I might be able to get rid of next (I suspect that this is not terribly healthy).

So once I'd purged the low-hanging fruit (because there really is no point keeping CDs you don't want to listen to), I decided to put the brakes on and enjoy what I had left, rather than keep forcing myself to find reasons to get rid of more. This turned out to be a brilliant idea. From putting one of my remaining CDs on in the morning to digging out my old vinyl and asking my dad to repair my record player, to making the effort to actually use one of the lipsticks I'd decided to keep, the acts themselves were fun and uplifting, and engaging with my possessions instead of just having them hanging around waiting to eventually be decluttered increased their value to me. It also made me slow right down and savour what I was doing. Appreciating – and using – what you have is key to not continually wanting more.

A simple way to feel better in your own skin is to be true to yourself. I didn't find it as easy as it sounds, but through baby steps – learning to say 'no', speaking my mind rather than hiding my feelings, letting go of clothes I didn't really feel comfortable wearing – I found that striving to be more authentic did wonders for my self-esteem.

When I was in my early teens, sharing clothes was pretty normal. It was exciting when my best friend Topaz got a bag of clothes handed down from her older, trendy neighbour, because I knew she'd give me what she didn't want and probably let me borrow the rest if I pleaded enough. My mum and I used to borrow each other's clothes too. Sometimes we even gave them back.

Nowadays, it's not so common to borrow a mate's dress to wear to a party. But for me on my shopping ban, having a community of friends and relatives I could call on to help out was heartwarming and uplifting, not to mention it saved me a penny or two.

When our electric whisk spluttered and died halfway through Dai making our son's first birthday cake, I called my friend Rose – she lived five minutes away, was a fellow mum so likely to be awake at such a silly time on a Sunday morning, and given her perfect house and propensity for holding coffee mornings, I felt sure she had a set of beaters we could borrow. And she came up trumps, saving us from a two-hour wait for the shops to open so we could have the cake ready in time for the party. (And she even said we could keep the beaters! What a woman.)

Topaz lent me a pair of smart shoes for an evening out, and we now have an agreement whereby we share the shoes – mostly they live with me, unless called upon by Topaz for an occasion, thus saving us both from needing to buy any more nude wedding-guest shoes for quite some time.

When lockdown started, I asked Alice, a hardcore movie buff, if she could lend me some family-friendly DVDs to get me and the Spud through those long afternoons. She dropped off a stack of DVDs on her way to work – along with her Disney+ password.

At first, I felt awkward and a bit weird asking for stuff, until I realised that it opened a door for people to ask me for things in return. This year I have lent and borrowed items from irons and plungers to books and hairdressing scissors, and therefore we have all saved a) money and b) resources, because rather than having one of everything each, we are sharing what we have.

I'm pleased to say as well that, as well as sharing, my friends and I do a lot of swapping. Maternity wear, baby clothes and toys have done the rounds from mum to mum in our group, saving us each a small fortune. And when we have a clear out, we have developed the habit of rehoming the clothes with a friend rather than plonking them straight into the charity shop.

Sometimes this has come in extremely helpful – just before my planned clothing swap in January 2020, my friend Ana was living in a camper van, which was stolen from a supermarket car park with all her possessions inside. Under my stairs at the time was a huge stash of clothes – spare items from all I had been given by Topaz, Bel and Alice, plus bags of things that had been given to me for the swap party. After making sure no one minded, I was able to go through it all and sort out an emergency stop-gap wardrobe for Ana.

I've noted before that the generosity of friends had helped me out of a tight spot during my ban, and I really feel now that being able to help each other out – and ask for help (and nick each other's clothes) – has brought us closer, and created a feeling of community. With the added bonus of being kinder to the environment. It's not exactly ground-breaking, but I was so out of the habit of asking for what I needed (when I could just buy it) that people's willingness to share came as a lovely surprise.

If you have read this far and relate to much of what I have said, I strongly feel you should consider doing a shopping ban of your own – it's a challenge I honestly think everyone can learn something from. If, however, you really can't face that, another experiment you could try is to pick a category of your belongings – books, clothing or make-up, for example – and try not to buy any more until something in that category actually needs replacing. You may be surprised by how much more you have than you actually need. For example, I was amazed to discover at the end of my first year that I had only worn out a single pair of socks, and still had more than ten remaining bottles of body lotion!

Here are a few of the most important things I have learned since I started trying to quit shopping:

1. Browsing leads to spending. Don't make it easy for them to keep you hooked. Put down your phone. My life became so much better when I stopped feeling obligated to compare every dress on ASOS.

2. You don't lose anything by not buying something.

3. There isn't One True Garment that will reveal and encapsulate your identity.

4. You can't shop your way to a sense of self. In fact, overshopping was part of what eroded my sense of self in the first place.

5. Use and value what you already have.

6. At the end of your life, you won't wish you'd spent more time shopping.

7. Express yourself through your actions, not your purchases.

8. Take inventory. Counting your stuff is not the most fun way to spend time, but it's harder to convince yourself you really need another T-shirt if you know you already have 63 T-shirts. (Yes, actual number. Have I not mentioned I have an overshopping problem?)

9. Consider your priorities. What are you giving up if you keep spending your money on unnecessary trinkets? A house deposit? That trip you've always wanted to take? Your security or peace of mind? What if you saved that money instead? One of the best tools at my disposal to curb my overshopping is very simple – I write down, each day, everything I have spent. Every month I add it up into categories – for example groceries, bills, gifts, cosmetics, books, clothes. This helps me see where I'm overspending (e.g., is too much money disappearing into the clothes or takeaway category every month?) and means I can't hide my habits from myself. (I also write down my ingoings, and how much I save. Obviously,

the idea is to have more going in than coming out, but that's not always how it goes!) I could name several people who bin their bank statements without opening them who could probably benefit from doing this. If the very idea makes you shudder, you probably could too. It's not about shame, judgement or beating yourself up. It's about gentle honesty, facing up to your actual behaviours, and deciding whether your spends are really in line with your priorities or not.

10. Don't broadcast everything. A private life is a happy life. I used to pour myself into social media in the name of authenticity and then always felt I had to live up to the image I was creating. Your choices become limited when you feel you should be promoting or explaining them to an audience. Deciding to be more mysterious was one of my best decisions to date.

11. Let go of perfect. I learned during wedding planning that perfection is a tyrant. Embrace 'good enough' and be liberated. My hair, my skin, my smile, my wardrobe – not perfect, but good enough, and that makes me happy every day. If you let go of perfect, you only have to meet your own standards – not society's, not Instagram's. (If your own standards still feel too high, can you try to see yourself how your friends and loved ones see you? Beyond facial features and body shape, true beauty is in the way you light up, the way you talk, smile, laugh, move.)

Chapter 7

The Year of Being Myself

So, 2021... After the Shitshow Formerly Known As 2020, I'll admit I was reluctant to get too excited about what might be in store. However, this year, I decided to change tactics a little with my shopping ban. I'd basically stopped doing anything that cost money (make-up, nail varnish, professional haircuts), generally citing environmental worries. I did eventually realise that one person not dyeing their hair was not going to change the world, and actually I was allowed to look nice.

I had hoped that cutting back my beauty routines would help me feel more confident and comfortable in my skin, and in some ways, it had – I'd come to like my own face without make-up, for example. But frankly I wanted to paint my nails without feeling guilty for being frivolous (yes, I'd beaten myself up over some weird things during the last year or so).

I'm not sure when being slightly more environmentally conscious tipped over in my head into complete self-denial, sackcloth and ashes, but I was definitely ready to move on from that now and find a balance between frugality, sustainability and actually being myself.

After I'd mentioned once or twice that I have the occasional wobble about being the 'worst dressed friend' or similar, I received such a sweet text from my dear friend Ana. She said, "Going back decades, I've always loved your sense of style and general randomosity of your clothes! We all get the little voice in the head telling us all the bad stuff, but tell your one that makes you worry about being the worst dressed where to go."

This gave me such a lift, and reminded me of the first clothing purchase I saved up for and bought myself – a pair of rainbow striped corduroy flares! I thought they were just the most beautiful, joyful things ever, and I loved them to pieces. No, they weren't tasteful, or 'cool', or even terribly flattering, but they make me smile even now when I think about them.

So this year, I wanted to relearn how to enjoy clothes and dress for myself again. This was not carte blanche for a big shopping spree! My finances were currently pretty stable, so I didn't have to pinch pennies quite as much, but I didn't want to end up right back where I started either! My goal was to really tune in to my gut feelings – and stop feeling guilty for wanting to enjoy clothes and have some fun with the way I look. Embrace the part of me that says rainbow trousers are a good idea (she's still in there, which is why I own purple tie dye dungarees).

It frustrated me that I'd not managed to complete my goal of 365 days without an unnecessary purchase, but I didn't like the way my brain turned 'not buying things I don't need' into 'wanting to wear clothes I actually like is consumerist'. I wanted to focus less on the not-shopping and more on what would come after – e.g., if I wasn't shopping, thinking about shopping, or planning my next purchase, where was I going to put all that creative energy?

Shopping, for me, has definitely been about expressing myself, via clothing, home decor, and other trinkets, so as well as learning to do that without a constant influx of the new, I also wanted to put the focus back on what I could produce instead of what I could consume. I didn't know in what way yet, I just knew that I didn't want my life to be forever revolving around stuff, whether buying it or not buying it. The most inspiring book I read in 2020 was *The Enchanted Life* by Sharon Blackie,[26] and it reminded me what a big part creativity used to play in my life, before Facebook and email and 24/7 online shopping filled up all the empty spaces.

I decided to make this a 'low-buy' rather than a no-shop year. I wanted to stop overshopping, but I also wanted to be able to purchase things relevant to my interests, or that otherwise brought value to my life, without it being a huge deal, or a source of guilt and stress. And I wanted to get out of the deprive-splurge-panic cycle I seemed to have ended up in.

Some of the tips I picked up on my Eco Thrift Crusade were great. Vinegar cleans everything and won't poison my child when he randomly licks stuff. Old baby vests with questionable food stains are fine for cleaning rags. But feeling drudge-like and glum with lank hair and ill-fitting clothes and shoes hardly made me an inspiring poster girl for the 'eco life'. I waffled between feeling smug for how 'anti-consumerist' I was now, and deeply uncomfortable when bumping into an old friend in town knowing I looked, well, a bit rough.

I'd always admired people who don't care much about their appearance – I like a bit of devil-may-care, and I think it's important to have more going on in your life than just thinking about your looks. But even people of my acquaintance who don't care much about clothes will buy things a) that they actually like, and b) that fit comfortably.

It was a bit of a newsflash to me that I actually deserved to take pleasure in the things I have around me. Just as I'd stopped doing my hair and nails out of eco guilt and rejection of 'vanity', I'd also forgotten somehow that I am allowed to want a nice house and a wardrobe of things I actually like. The panacea for overshopping isn't asceticism. I was inflicting a weird sort of penance on myself, and yeah, okay, my shopping behaviour has at times been selfish and greedy, but being a martyr didn't exactly improve the situation.

This last couple of years I'd tried really hard to embrace anti-consumerism and simple living, but I kept tripping over my love of clothes, adornments and other little luxuries. This made me feel quite disappointed, but it did seem to be in my nature. I could moderate it and choose not to make a purchase, but I couldn't seem to just stop being interested in my style, even when I felt convinced that it made me shallow or silly.

I knew that I could indulge my enjoyment of dressing up without shopping for new things all the time, but persistently telling myself that I must not shop seemed to be shooting myself in the foot a little. I was tired of guilt and self-analysis and for feeling like a terrible person because I liked sparkly nails and quirky jewellery and was not a combination of Swampy and a Buddhist monk.

I'd just had enough of the feeling that I was somehow cut off from the flow of normal life because I had to second-guess every purchase I thought of making. Maybe I could get close to the present, focused, conscious, creative life that I wanted without imposing a total moratorium on new items?

Part II
...Stay for the Druidry

Chapter 8

The Weird, the Wild and the Woo-Woo

I suppose you could say that at this point in my path I was a lapsed Pagan. I've dabbled (the most accurate term in my case, I'm afraid) in assorted branches of Pagan religion since my pre-teens. Now, due to my increased interest in and connection with nature, history, folklore and more, I'd been taking another look at these faiths and traditions. My intuition suggested that introducing a spiritual aspect into my life would help to fill the void inside that I'd previously papered over with excessive shopping.

This void was not the gaping darkness it had been. These last couple of years had done me good – I'd picked up a variety of creative hobbies, renewed connections with family and friends, and even with the wider world through activism, and disconnected somewhat from my gadgets. I was not as painfully self-conscious, not as distracted, and not as prone to constant comparison. Lately I'd picked up my long-neglected yoga and meditation practice too. It was a bit sporadic, but it helped. Looking deeper into the spiritual now felt like a natural next step – one I'd avoided for a long time, for fear of looking or sounding 'woo-woo', upsetting the die-hard sceptics amongst my family and friends, or simply feeling worried that I didn't know what I was doing, and might not find what I'd always felt I was looking for.

(Do you ever have the feeling that you're following a trail of breadcrumbs through life? Since childhood I've felt 'nudges' or seen signs that I do my best to follow, trying to piece together a bizarre map of coincidences, hunches, feelings, and notes from a plethora of old books. More and more lately I found myself musing on the saying, "That which you seek is seeking you.")

Why Paganism? Because it felt right to me. I grew up with remedies from the herb garden and food from the hedgerows. When I walked on the land, I felt part of a huge and intricate web. The more I saw and came to know of nature, the more it felt miraculous, magical. I felt my ancestors, my history, my connection to the soil and the chalk and the bones of the land. In our home, we began to celebrate the turning of the seasons by marking the solstices and traditional fire festivals – I thought it was a good way for all of us to feel connected to nature, and the little one enjoyed gathering greenery and blossoms to decorate the table for our feasts.

Once when I was young, I stayed up all night reading poetry, and the dawn chorus and the breaking light seemed like such a gift, such a wondrous and incredible thing, that for a short time I thought I had found God, and became a devoted churchgoer. I could still feel that sense of awe and joy, of reverence, for the natural world, but I no longer felt that it fitted within the framework of patriarchal Abrahamic religion. That was just the only frame of reference I had at the time, the only hook on which I could hang such emotions and experience.

I'm also psychic. Or perhaps that's a bit strong – intuitive, or sensitive, might be a better term. In really small ways usually – dreams that come true being the most common. I also briefly had a sideline in telling fortunes at secondary school for fifty pence a pop, until my accuracy was denounced as 'creepy' and one girl spread a rumour I could tell you when you were going to die (spoiler: no I can't). I'd never made any real effort to work with it or hone it – in fact I'd generally suppressed it (that fear of being too woo-woo, again) – but every now and again I get something a bit more dramatic and difficult to explain, such as the way I met my first serious boyfriend. I woke up one Saturday morning, and could 'see', in my head, exactly what was going to happen that day. Not as a vision, but the knowledge was just *there*, whole and complete.

I got into action before my rational mind could talk me out of it. I got up and dressed, tidied my room, took my guitar out of the cupboard and stood it in the corner. I wrote my phone number on a slip of card and put it in my pocket. I walked to my friend Ana's house down the street, and together we walked to a house we'd never visited before. My now-ex was in the garden. We looked at each other. Ana and I walked away. In my head, I was counting down – and on cue, he came running after us. I gave him my number.

An hour or so later we were all hanging out in my conspicuously tidy room. The new guy was playing *Basket Case* by Green Day on my guitar. We were together for over a decade. In fact, part of the reason I stuck out the relationship for so long was because of the circumstances in which we met – I felt perhaps we were capital-F Fated. Now I suspect I simply wanted a boyfriend so much that I accidentally manifested one.

It's not that I think this kind of experience is a prerequisite for choosing a Pagan path, but I do feel that these traditions provide a good structure for learning how to use and channel this 'ability', so that – I hope – it can become something I can work with and direct rather than being something that just happens to me.

I've had other weird experiences – both in similar vein, and very much not – which have shaped my world view in a big way. I don't often discuss any of this, as I know even my most supportive friends might be disbelieving, and I don't want to feel I have to excuse or justify what I have felt and experienced. But I was done with pretending that such experiences and feelings don't have a huge influence on who I am. I didn't want to suppress this part of myself any more – I wanted to embrace it, and go deeper.

As a teenage would-be Wiccan, I very much followed a Pagan-by-numbers approach. I bought a book that told me the names of some deities, and the right words to say for this or that ritual, and which herbs or coloured candles to buy. I dutifully followed the steps, but I never *felt* anything. It was like shouting into an abyss.

Now I was a bit older, it was obvious why this approach didn't work. You can't just read a name in a book and tell yourself to believe in it. This time around, I intended to listen to my intuition, read widely, get my hands muddy, and find a path based on what I know, feel, experience and believe. It was time to get my woo-woo on.

In March I started thinking about my thirtieth birthday, which was coming up in September. I wanted to do something special to mark the date, but I didn't fancy throwing a party and all the hassle that would entail. Besides, after a year in lockdown I wasn't feeling very people-y. I decided that what I wanted above all was something that would symbolically mark, for me, the closing of my twenties and the beginning of a new decade. A ceremonial ending, or healing, so that I could leave some of the real low points from the last decade safely behind me – a way to say, *that's done now, and you can move forward.*

Almost on a whim, I sent an email to Goddess House in Glastonbury,[27] enquiring whether they were taking bookings for their holistic treatments and healings. I told them a little about myself and asked whether they could recommend a treatment; the lady who answered sent me some links to their information pages and suggested I see whether I felt drawn to anything.

I noticed that they listed a deluxe treatment called Brighde's Blessing, and although I felt silly acknowledging this, it seemed a bit like a sign. Brighde is one of many names for the Irish goddess Brigid, goddess of smithcraft, healing and poetry. I've always felt drawn to Brigid and fascinated by her legends – I decided to go out on a limb and make the booking.

Once it was confirmed for the day before my birthday, I

arranged an overnight stay near Glastonbury with Dai and the Spud, and told Dai that on my birthday itself I wanted to do the one thing we'd run out of time to do on our last visit – walk to the top of Glastonbury Tor.

The Tor, according to its National Trust webpage,[28] has been a spiritually significant site for over 1,000 years. Though little is known for certain, there are many legends about the Tor, including that it may be the Isle of Avalon,[29] the entrance to the underworld,[30] that it has been sacred to worshippers of an earth goddess.[31]

One of the many theories holds that the top of the Tor is the centre of the labyrinth formed by the surrounding terraces, which may have been designed to lead the spiritual seeker on a meditative journey into the interior self.[32] It seemed like a pretty good place to start my next decade, anyway.

Almost from the day I made the booking, it seemed like something changed inside me. I'd already been becoming more aware of nature since I cut down on my shopping and my phone use, but now that I had allowed a chink in my habitual skepticism and accepted even the slightest, vaguest possibility of a goddess, everything seemed suddenly more vibrant, more wondrous. Every day I made time to watch the sunset – it seemed like a gift, a miracle.

I was trepidatious, but excited. It felt like the beginning of something new, an opening up, emerging into a new way of being. Yes, I'd approached Paganism before, but it turned out that for me there was a world of difference between deciding to believe something – wanting to believe it – and slowly opening oneself to the actual experiencing of it. In this new quieter, private life I had carved out, I had time and space to try things, to read widely, to go deeply into the most basic practices. To slowly form something that could be rich and real, rather than crashing about adopting a mystical persona, buying a gazillion witchy trinkets, and trying to be beyond reproach of 'gatekeepers' by looking at all times as if I knew what I was doing, whether or not I had the faintest idea.

I started to put my feelers out, reading more books and browsing the internet to see if I could find a path that felt like it might lead me somewhere I wanted to go. Sometimes the feeling that change was afoot – or simply that I was just being a big weirdo – made me get scared, and think about 'calling the whole thing off', so to speak – just go back to being 'normal'. Wasn't it enough for me that I had quit shopping in New Look et al, that I lobbied my MP so regularly on environmental issues that I could hear his eyes rolling in the distance every time I pressed send? Did I really have to keep pushing myself further outside the boundaries of the mainstream?

But the other feelings were stronger. I was sick of suppressing, ignoring, and cutting myself off from a whole section of life that was calling to me. Realistically, I had already seen and experienced things that I couldn't explain away with rationalism, so it was no use worrying about being 'out there' – it was already too late for me! I determined not to let fear or embarrassment hold me back any longer – not with clothes, not with speaking my mind, not with being creative, not with spirituality.

As I researched, I kept up with my meditation practice. I tried to remain present, to notice my feelings, and to be honest with people. I continued spending time outside every single day, watching the sunset, observing the plants and the wildlife and how they changed and interacted. I continued to grow my own herbs and started to work with divination, using my oracle cards, another practice which I had let slip a long time ago. I didn't yet have a handle on where I was going with this, but I kept reminding myself of my new mantra: baby steps, being true to myself, not being afraid.

There are a number of reasons why I'm not very good at being green. Whilst I did – do – my best, I still often felt like a beginner at these lifestyle changes, and I've made more than a handful of bad decisions along the way. I console myself with the fact that I alone won't make any huge difference one way or the other, but as someone who cares about nature and the environment, and who wants to leave a safe and thriving planet for future generations, I still feel that it's worth trying to bring my lifestyle in line with my values.

In some areas, I felt like I was doing okay. I'd hosted a successful clothing swap party (pre-COVID!) and look forward to doing so again one day. We clean our house with reusable cloths and white vinegar, we use cloth wipes for the little one's bum (he doesn't like wearing the reusable nappies, though, which I wish I could have predicted before I bought them as they're hardly cheap. And I don't know if the staff at his nursery next year will be willing to use cloth wipes, but I'll certainly ask), and I continue to volunteer for Greenpeace. I use an eco-friendly natural deodorant, and boy, it took a long time to find one that was natural, effective, and doesn't contain baking soda, to which I'm sensitive. My hair dye is henna; for laundry I use an eco-ball with a touch of Dr Bronner's if it's Dai's work gear or baby poop; I have a safety razor so I don't use disposables. We have a sustainable loo roll subscription. I'm on a green energy tariff (I use USwitch to get the best deals). So it's not all bad!

But there are still a lot of changes I was struggling with. My biggest weakness – and this won't surprise you! – is that I still found it really hard not to shop for new clothes. Even though I didn't need any! It's a problem. Yes, I was buying from much better companies, and I no longer spent my entire bank account every month (hooray) so things had distinctly improved. Fashion is such a polluting industry, though, that I really wanted to stop shopping when I didn't actually need to be.

I found it hugely frustrating that others find it comparatively easy not to clothes shop. Topaz had only bought a handful of second-hand items on eBay since her last big clear-out, which was the previous year. Whereas I seemed to be convinced that I'd miss out on some magical item that would, I don't know, round out my personality and give my life meaning?

I've made the mistake of trying to buy my way to sustainability, spending a fortune on organic veg boxes and reusable nappies and fancy matching cloths and zero waste bras (okay, I actually really recommend these, they're from Pethau Bach on Etsy[33] and they're brilliant and gorgeous. They also come in a breastfeeding style, which is what I currently wear) and jute washing up cloths and organic toothpaste and so on and so on, which blew a chunk of my finances and turned out to be completely unnecessary in a lot of cases. You can use old cotton T-shirts for cleaning rags, you don't actually need a colour coordinated set. I've also tried to do the opposite and stop spending any unnecessary moneys ever, but I went too far in my Eco Thrift Crusade and felt like a right joyless old frump; in the end it was a relief to run out and buy some nail polish. So, as usual, extremes are counter-productive, at least for me.

For a while I felt tired of the whole thing – I'd lost any sense of what the point was, and the ever-present temptation of shopping my way to fulfilment (or at least a sort of pleasant-ish numbness) was starting to seem a far more tantalising prospect. Funnily enough, it was my rekindled interest in Paganism which revived my interest in green and simple living. I say funnily enough because my previous forays into various Pagan paths have involved purchasing a lot of fancy implements and setting up elaborate altars only to feel disheartened and move on after a couple of months.

This time I bought no athames, pentacles, incense, altar cloths, crystals, divination decks, herbs, Goddess statues, wands, runes, singing bowls, ritual robes, goofer dust, crystal balls, besoms, black mirrors, candles or anything else! Instead I took my own advice – spent time daily in nature, kept up my meditation practice and did a bit of online research.

I came across a description of Druidry on the Druid Network website that stopped me in my tracks, as it seemed very close to what I'd been feeling and experiencing myself. To just hit a couple of high points for you:

> "The path that defines the activities of the Druid often starts with the acquisition of awareness and connection, sometimes born from the skill of observation.
> There is no part of life where a Druid is not engaging with their gods, ancestors and the environment – lighting a fire in the hearth, tending the garden, caring for children, watching the sunrise," from the Druid Network article, *What Do Druids Do?*. [34]

I loved that this was a way of being in the world that would allow me to see my mundane responsibilities as sacred. But I wanted to know more about Druidry before I could say for sure that it was the path for me, so I needed to get my hands on some books and look into it further. At this point I was excited – it seemed that I had found a down-to-earth philosophy of living that could add meaningfulness to my environmentally-based choices and depth to my experience of the world.

The Order of Bards, Ovates and Druids[35] offers a highly recommended correspondence course that I was intrigued by, not least because you're assigned a mentor whom you can plague with questions (Dai can attest to the fact that I was full of annoying spiritual questions). I'd also been reading some Druid blogs (Druid blogs!) and, well, isn't it great when you find someone else articulating things you've been thinking and feeling?

So that's where I was at. Imperfectly green but doing my best, intrigued by Druidry, excited by possibilities (and overfond of parentheses).

Since I realised the calming, uplifting effect that walking in nature had on me, I started spending more and more time outside. The Spud benefited from this too – he loves to be out in the fresh air. As well as our everyday walks, when the weather was good, we packed a picnic into my backpack and headed out on a longer expedition.

In recent years I'd moved from the country village where I grew up to a council estate in the suburbs. There was a bit of adjustment required when we arrived in this grey terrace, but soon I discovered there was a nature reserve behind the estate with a river running through it. Now the Spud was bigger and could walk further, we could hike across the fields to the woodlands I used to walk in when I was growing up.

Each year more land is sold to the developers, and more of the fields I used to play in are swallowed by the urban sprawl, but it was still relatively easy to scratch off the thin veneer of civilisation and find ourselves far from anywhere, between Roman roads and Old Straight Tracks, copses and hedgerows and sun-dappled glades of celandine and primrose. You could still see the progress of mankind in the ploughed fields and tumbledown barns, the glint of a beer bottle in the nettles, the pylon stalking unexpectedly across the horizon like an invader from another time. But it felt for all the world as though we were alone on the edges of things, where something magical might still happen.

I belong here, I found myself thinking, as the Spud and I shared a sandwich and a drink of water in the shade of a hedge. Looking out over the fields I could see the straight, tree-lined cut of a Roman road. I'd walked that road with my mother as a child, and for years after I'd had a recurring dream about it, a cloaked rider on a dark horse pounding down the hill towards me.

The Spud and I followed the footpath across the centre of the field. Vast clouds sailed across the sky like zeppelins, sending shadows chasing over the ploughed earth. I felt like Tiffany

Aching walking on the Chalk.[36] *Perhaps*, I thought idly, *if I were ever to set up an altar again, I might do better to have some of these flints than some fancy shiny imported crystals, no matter how pretty. After all, this ground here is what I'm made of. This chalk and flint may as well be my bones.*

My mother's maiden name comes from 'Free', and there have been Frees here, and in the surrounding area, since records began. (I did some digging into my ancestry recently, and other than my paternal grandmother who was from Bornholm – and her ancestors, back to the 1700s at least, adding a strain of Norse to my makeup that I'm quite proud of – my family looks to be of Anglo-Saxon descent on both sides.)

Just as I was musing about flints on my altar, the Spud caught hold of my jeans and offered me a huge flattish oval specimen that he had prised out of the dirt of the path. Crouching beside him, I turned it over in my hands, and caught my breath. The underside of the flint was covered in sparkling crystal that glittered in the sunlight. *Wow*, I thought. *Okay. I can take a hint.*

This is far from the strangest thing that has happened to me out on the wild edges of this land. Nor am I the only one who can tell stories about this area. Britain on the whole is a strange country with an equally strange history, which is why I love it so much.

The street I grew up on was at the edge of the village and ended in farmland. There was a big pasture at the end of the road, which was bordered on the far side by a very old narrow footpath known locally as the cinder track.

One evening when I was about eight or nine, my friend Alec and I were sitting with our backs against someone's garage door on the edge of the pasture, talking rubbish and looking out over the fields as the sun went down. We both saw, at the same moment, a figure striding along the cinder track towards the village.

I remember looking at Alec to make sure he was seeing it too, and my own fear was reflected in his eyes. The dark figure – a black silhouette – was taller than the straggly trees that bordered the footpath, making it ten, eleven feet tall or more. Its arms were unnaturally long, reaching past its knees. And even from this distance, impossibly, we could both see its eyes, which were deep red, glowing like hot coals. And there was this... *feeling*, seeping from it like mist, a *malevolence*.

Without a word to each other we both bolted, ran for our houses, leaving dust in our wake.

Sometimes, walking in the woods with my little boy, I feel like I've stepped sideways out of the flow of what is deemed to be 'normal life'. There are days when I'm so enmeshed in the System – earn your money, pay your bills, check your emails, go to the supermarket, watch TV, work work, rush rush, veg out, repeat – that getting out of it seems impossible. I look at those I know who live in vans and on boats, who drift on the wind and the tide at whim, and I can no longer figure out a way to join them.

But I'm not sold on the other way of living either, and I feel that keenly when we're wandering on the edges. I feel a gulf between me and the world of Friends re-runs and hair straighteners, Love Island and eyelash curlers and Primark... so much that seems meaningless. I feel more and more like I'm looking at that world from somewhere else, and it's a language that I don't understand any more.

Sometimes it's alienating to believe in magic and monsters when most of those around you are existing in a different reality. But I've seen what I've seen and felt what I've felt, and the flint of the land, thousands of years old, is in my bones. Strange things still happen on the Old Straight Tracks, even as the sound of traffic encroaches and the pylons march on across the landscape. The weird and the wild are still out there, beyond this 'civilised' existence we've trapped ourselves in, if you know where to look.

It dawned on me eventually that I seemed to be having a spiritual experience. I couldn't explain away or ignore these feelings I was having – every time I found myself in nature, I was almost drunk, giddy with awe. I was suddenly aware that I was connected to everything else, part of nature, that the same energy was coursing through everything. The sense that something bigger was immanent, was reaching out to me, made me almost euphoric.

Every time I sensed my protective shell of skepticism rising up around me, all I had to do was go outside, and the ground beneath my feet and the wind on my face soothed me again. I kept expecting this sense of being connected to fade away or reveal itself as a figment of imagination, but it stayed and stayed and stayed. I had an impression not only of benign-ness, but of patience. It was both scary and not-scary at the same time.

The insistence of the feeling, its undeniability, was unsettling to me, as I had steered so far away from trying to be 'New Agey'. I'd donated my Tarot cards to the charity shop. I sneered at people who believed in crystal healing. And now here I was, reeling delightedly before the face of the mystical. Yet at the same time, what a joy it was, and a relief – I was right, *I was right*, there has been magic all along, the ground is nearly humming with it, all I had to do was put down my gadgets, go outside and *notice*. I felt my mind and heart unfolding like reverse origami. How did everyone not feel like this all the time?

I was musing recently on how I'd managed to go from the relatively simple concept of a shopping ban to finding myself interested in Earth-based spirituality and considering a course in Druidry over the space of two years. But actually I found that when I looked back it was quite easy to track the progression, a sort of spiralling journey from needing to do something to take my mind off shopping and get out of my own head; spending more time outside; falling back in love with the Earth and trying to live greener; taking up foraging and gardening, as well as environmental campaigning, which made me feel more and more connected to the Earth. This sense of connectedness then led me to start exploring Paganism – and here we are. Adding a spiritual or philosophical element to the green(ish) life, for me, helps to make it even more meaningful and fulfilling. The mythopoetic worldview[37] ties into my lifelong love of the imagination and the liminal, and my staunch belief that all we can perceive with our limited human senses is far from being all there is.

However, knowing my tendency to cling to labels, not to mention my propensity for theatricality (I was goth for the better part of a decade – being at least a little bit theatrical is practically a job description), I determined to be slow and methodical about my studies, to make sure that what I was doing felt right for me and aligned with my actual lived experience (you can tell me all you want that amethyst and clear quartz are good for headaches, for example, and maybe for some people they are, but I might as well rub a custard cream on my forehead for all the good it does. Just because something is written in a book doesn't make it true for me).

I also didn't want to do what I often do and believe everything I read without question, especially on the internet. Accepting an animistic worldview is an easy step for me – hello, I am a person who, as a child, brought home sticks that 'looked lonely' – I'm pretty much there already. However, I'm not going to go 'full Glastonbury' as Dai calls it and start thinking I might be a Starseed – I'm definitely not. Reminder to brain: believing some stuff that makes sense to you and fits with what you know and have experienced does not equal believing everything ever espoused by anyone who owns a pentagram necklace.

I'd also found that a lot of associations, groups, and individuals offered mentorship or teaching for spiritual seekers, but often at astronomical prices. This made me wary, as it was hard from the outside to discern who was genuine and who was grasping – what could be truly helpful or meaningful, and what was a money-spinner. I had to remember to keep checking in with my gut feelings – and I quickly found that if I felt in doubt, or worried, or stressed, the cure was to drop everything and go outside. The full moon hanging low over the river in a pale lilac sky soon put me back to rights.

But it was that theatrical tendency of mine I was particularly on guard against. I've mentioned before that my previous forays into Paganism have been accompanied by much swishing of velvet and clinking of esoteric jewellery. I'm really only ever a heartbeat away from putting on elf ears and a flower crown and flouncing into the sunset in a flutter of tie dye and a jingle of silvery bells. What I didn't want to do this time around was buy into a Pagan 'image' without doing any real work, stock up on esoteric-looking goodies as though magic was something you could buy (to paraphrase Terry Pratchett[38]); or worse, spend time on social media showing all my friends how earthy and spiritual I am...

This is where I need to watch my step. I understand that for many people, online communities, based around social media or otherwise, are very valuable. This is just as true within the Pagan community (the Resistance Witches with the 'Hex Trump' campaign are a memorable example!). And by no means does enjoying fashion (of any kind) or posting a selfie mean that someone is not participating in something real or valuable or meaningful.

But I have found that for me personally, it detracts. Maintaining an image, whether through fashion or an Instagram feed, takes energy, time and work. Energy, time and work that I could better use studying, or writing, improving my focus, tending my herbs (or my son), or just going down to the river. If I break away from that to craft a good photo, my focus is split;

I am not as peaceful, the connection falters; some of the benefit is lost. Likewise if I am worrying about my hair, or concerned about snagging my skirt.

Dai and I also saw, on our last trip to Glastonbury, a fair number of what Dai describes as 'Insta-witches' – a lot of the more 'mystical' areas in the village, such as the beautiful Chalice Well, were surrounded by people taking photos for social media – we couldn't actually get near the Well on that particular visit as two women had colonised the area to set up a jewellery display which they were photographing. And we queued for half an hour to drink from the Red Spring as we had to wait for another bevy of phone-clutching mystics to finish setting up crystal grids and photographing their bare feet. (I don't intend to cast aspersions or be snarky! But from an observer's perspective, it seemed... like posturing.)

It certainly got me thinking about my own approach – I really wanted to avoid taking a 'does it look good and are people watching?' approach to spirituality. I'd been reading a book by Penny Billington called *The Path of Druidry*,[39] and when I read some reviews on Good Reads I noted that a handful of people were irritated by a remark she makes in one of the early chapters, where she suggests that a Druid should look fairly normal and dress unnoticeably, as this would give them more freedom to get on with their work, and that spending time creating a deliberately wise or eccentric image takes energy that could be better spent elsewhere.[40]

Now, I can totally see why this didn't suit some people – 'fitting in' isn't really something I'm big on either. But my daily nature-walking wear of jeans and T-shirts is, well, pretty invisible. And for me, this was such a refreshing thing to read – an instant antidote to the itchy eBay bidding finger (step away from the Jordash dresses).

I am someone who was recently described by a dear friend as "a New Age hippy... I think of you like one of those paper dolls, you mix it up and try different things, but your base setting is hippy fairy". (Naturally I'm delighted by this description.) So, believe me when I say, I can easily devote my time to being 'self-consciously eccentric'. I could start my own Instagram account of woodland selfies where I never look directly at the camera because I'm very mysterious and bohemian, or rip up flowers and fungi so I can take a photo of my hand holding them. Or, I can dress in a way that's pleasing enough, comfortable, and still allows me to tromp through muddy fields, and just get on with it! It was a relief to have it spelt out for me that clothes do not maketh the Druid. It may not be even vaguely an issue for those who do not have my preoccupation with style and shopping, but it was a huge deal for me.

I decided that balance is, as it often is, the key. My dramatic skirts had their place – when we visited our favourite canalside pub for a pint of ale, or roaming the streets of Burley or Glastonbury. But when I want to be able to crawl into hedges, cross streams or move through woodland, it's sensible coat and shoes all the way. This probably seems really obvious to you! But I, for whatever reason (gothy theatrical tendencies?) benefit from a reminder.

Chapter 9

Connections

I was an outdoorsy, free-range child, but as a teen, things changed. As I grew older and spent more and more time on my appearance, I also spent more and more time online. I was the girl who wore six-inch heels to walk the dog. I wore a full face of make-up to stay indoors on the computer. It just became my new normal. I lost touch with the previous version of me who played amongst the bluebells and always had grass stains on her knees. Eventually I started to avoid doing anything that might smudge my eyeliner, interfere with my hair extensions or damage my lace petticoats. I stopped going swimming or to the beach. It actually got to the point when the breeze on my skin felt irritating – annoying and alien. I preferred to stay indoors, where the temperature was regulated and nothing might mess up my hair. Chatrooms, blogs and forums were my 'real world'.

I realise that in a lot of ways I was an extreme case. Luckily this bizarre phase only lasted a short while. But I'll never forget feeling disturbed by the slightest of breezes! Now I'm more like my mum who, come rain, shine, storms or snow, always went to the back doorstep first thing upon waking, and sat on the step wrapped in her dressing gown, looking into the garden with her cup of tea. That peaceful time and connection with the outdoors is a great way to start the day refreshed and grounded, even if your toddler wants you to join in his persecution of the local woodlouse population rather than drink your coffee in peace.

With the benefit of hindsight, I can see now how lucky I was to be able to have such an outdoorsy childhood. We were able to rent a house in the village, which we might not otherwise have had access to, as my parents worked for the landowners. This provided a brilliant place to grow up – surrounded by woodlands and meadows, I could play unsupervised but safe from traffic, and I was able to range further as I got older. Of course not every child has access to this much unspoilt nature, particularly not nowadays as we try desperately to house our growing population and provide the infrastructure that they need.

We now live in a digital age. Many well-meaning friends and family have said things to me like, "Not to worry, soon you can get your little one a tablet, and then you won't have to do so much with him." I absolutely could plonk him in front of a screen for several hours a day, but as we've learned when we've fallen back on that easy option before, we all suffer. His mood suffers, his behaviour suffers, and bedtime becomes an all-out battle. So we keep screen time to a minimum – just an episode of one of his favoured shows now and again, usually if Dai's working and I need to cook dinner without small hands trying to investigate all the hots and sharps.

If it hadn't been for the Spud, I'm not sure whether I would ever have rediscovered my love of the outdoors. He's an extremely active child – I once took him to a class for lively toddlers and he ran rings around all the others before effecting an escape through a door one of the other mums had left open whilst looking at her phone. I had to hurdle chairs, bags, and other people's children to catch him before he could find his way out into the street.

To keep his energy levels under control so we can have relatively calm days, he has a minimum of an hour's walk around the neighbourhood. Every day, rain or shine. In the warmer months, he spends more time in the garden than in the house. Had I not been a parent, I might have spent a good chunk of 2020 under the duvet, or vegetating in front of Netflix. As it was, every day we spent our allotted hour down on the nature reserve, avoiding other people and enjoying the birdsong, and we've kept up the habit. If the weather's bad, we often don't see anyone else around. On rainy days, we put on our wellies and waders and go splashing down the river, just us and the ducks.

I recently read about 1000 Hours Outside,[41] which encourages kids and parents to match screen time with time in nature, and I've kept this in the back of my mind ever since – on those days when I struggle to feel enthusiastic about rebuilding the leaf pile for him to jump into for the 97th time, or when he's leading me further away from home just as I'm starting to think about checking my email. Every hour we spend wandering woodland paths and back alleys is another hour closer to that epic 1000 hours.

The fact is that although I no longer live in an idyllic village, I want my son to have the same interest in the outdoors that I have. The sad truth is that we now live in one of the most nature-depleted countries in the world.[42] One in seven of the UK's native species face extinction.[43] Just 13% of the UK's land area has tree cover – compared to a 35% average over the rest of Europe.[44] And if my generation raise our children indoors, staring at screens, things can only get worse.

Not only are we depriving our children of a vast array of joys and wonders if we fail to encourage this connection, but it's bad for the rest of the ecosystem too. Children won't care about what they don't know. In our increasingly industrialized society, facing a deeply uncertain future of extreme weather events, pandemics and climate chaos, further alienation from the world that sustains us will only further contribute to the modern view of nature as hostile and 'other' at best, and at worst a collection of meaningless resources to be plundered.

So, having come this far, I guess it's time I addressed an important question, for those of you who may not know: what is Druidry?

The standard answer amongst Druids is generally a variation on: well, there are almost as many answers to that as there are individual Druids. This was part of what intrigued me – I've never much fancied the idea of having a spiritual path prescribed for me. Believe it or not, I'm quite a private person, and I wanted to be able to explore this new realm of interconnection in my own way and in my own time.

Modern Druidry, I have come to understand, can be expressed commonly in two forms:

Reconstructionism, those who try to keep their rituals and practices as close as possible to how it is believed the original, ancient Druids would have done so.

Revivalism, those who take the little that we know about those long-ago Celtic folks (which really isn't much, as they passed down their history orally, and many of the existing written sources are from later time periods and rather unhelpfully contradict each other), plus some additions from the Druid Revival in the 1700-1800s, and apply it in a modern context, where it often may take on elements from other Pagan traditions, or even, in some instances, ideas from Eastern traditions such as Buddhism.

Views differ, again, as to whether Druidry is a religion or more of a philosophy – with its emphasis on love and respect for all beings, wisdom and creativity – and there are many Druids who also practise other religious paths alongside their Druidry, again running the gamut from varying forms of Paganism, through Christianity to Buddhism.

Typically Druids seek connection with the earth, their local landscapes in particular, and hold nature as sacred. An animistic worldview is common; many Druids are polytheists or pantheists. Often, Druids also believe in the existence of the Otherworld, a reality that may not be accessible by our traditional five senses but that we may see in meditation or dreams (or at times entirely by chance), and where we may go to rest when we die. Many

Druids also accept the idea of reincarnation or rebirth.

Some Druids practise alone and are known as solitary, or 'hedge' (or even 'feral') Druids; others meet in groups called groves to take part in rituals and celebrations. There are many Druid groups and orders worldwide who offer various teachings and courses as well as community; often these follow a format inspired by Celtic tradition wherein the student progresses through three grades – as Bard, Ovate and Druid.

This is a very basic, even simplistic overview – for more detail and greater understanding I would encourage you to investigate websites such as The Druid Network,[45] the British Druid Order,[46] and the Order of Bards, Ovates and Druids. I have also recommended several books in the Further Reading section at the back of this book. However, I hope this is enough to be getting on with!

As I learned more and continued to explore this ancient, modern philosophy, I kept looking for the catch. Something that would tell me, this path is not for you. I had tentatively – or not-so-tentatively – poked my nose into other faiths and spiritual traditions down the years, and after the initial spark of excitement, found no real connection – found myself following rote scripts without any real energy or focus – or uncovered an element here or there that didn't sit quite right with my personal values or understanding of the world.

But so far – no catch. Instead, that feeling of excitement began to blossom into a feeling of rightness. I tried not to get swept off my feet, to evaluate with a level head, but the more I read and studied, the more confident I began to feel about choosing to follow this road.

Now that I had allowed some small chinks in my armour – or, to put it better, now that I was becoming more aware and receptive – I began to experience a series of communications and coincidences that seemed to me to confirm that I was on the right track. It was astonishing to me – who had been seeking something since, well, as long as I can remember, with little success – to actually begin to have these experiences without conscious effort. It was as if, now that I was able to listen properly, something out there was ready to speak.

And yet at the same time, it was maddening. Firstly because it was hard to explain – to Dai, or to anyone. It's not as though I could provide concrete evidence of what was beginning to happen. The clouds did not part and a voice begin to speak; a figure of shimmering golden light did not manifest above my altar and bestow blessings. It was far more subtle, at first. A nudge here. An urge there. Easy to dismiss as happening entirely within my own mind; easy to write off and ignore, if I wanted to climb back into my cynical box.

The first time it happened, it was Beltane. I was at my altar, as I had begun to think about it – a beautiful handmade wooden chest that my dad had found and repaired many years earlier. I'd begun collecting items here that felt right – a glass bowl painted by a close friend; shells and leaves; my beautiful sparkling flint. I kept my oracle deck here, and I'd started sitting here most days to kind of 'check in', and try to meditate, or practise my pennywhistle.

As I was sitting, I felt a sort of – nudge. In my brain. An interest, a curiosity. Directed at my music box, sitting nearby on a bookshelf. (Given to me by Topaz, it plays Hedwig's Theme.) It was a fleeting sensation, but strong. Intense. Even so, I could have dismissed it. I almost did, in fact. *It's just a music box*, I thought. Then I paused. So what if it was all in my head? What would it cost me, to spend a few moments tinkling the music box?

So I did. And I felt delight. Laughter. I felt... connected to something. I let the music box sit on my altar for a long while after that.

I didn't tell Dai. What could I say? – "I think faeries are talking to me." Even I knew it sounded nuts. All the same, I was pretty excited.

At the time I was working my way studiously through *The Path Of Druidry*. When it had arrived in the post, I'd found a great horse chestnut leaf nestled between its pages, neatly pressed and perfectly intact, which made me smile. As I began to work through the book, I found that I had already, instinctively been doing many of the suggested exercises, before reading them. It was at this time that I received my crystal-encrusted flint whilst walking in the fields.

There was an experience that particularly astonished me at the time, but will be difficult to describe adequately. I was in the back seat of the car, travelling with Dai, his dad and the Spud, to a pub just over the county line to make some enquiries about hosting our wedding, which we were completely re-planning post-COVID – since our original venue turned out to be a no-go, we realised that this was a chance to arrange something a little more offbeat – the handfasting I had always secretly wanted.

It was an unseasonably hot day in April; the car windows were rolled down and the breeze streamed in. We were driving on winding roads I'd never travelled down before, and I felt a sensation on my arms – I described it to Dai, and later in my journal, as a 'cool, silvery tingle' on my skin. I knew that when I looked out of the window, there would be a river – and was quite disgruntled when I duly looked, only to find a metal railing and a copse of trees. Above and behind, a white horse outlined in chalk was poised mid-gallop upon the grassy hillside. But in moments, I found myself catching my breath as a ribbon of glistening blue unspooled from behind the trees and snaked away through the valley. I couldn't understand how I'd known it would be there.

I might have thought no more about this if I hadn't then later read in my trusty *Path Of Druidry* a description of magic that was very similar to what I had felt.[47] What I had experienced was more a physical sensation than a quality of light, but it was enough to keep me wondering!

Every now and again I had an off day, where I would waver, and ask myself, was I not being silly, with this interest in Druidry? Was I getting too into it? Could I not just be normal, go shopping, watch TV instead of getting obsessed by all this eco stuff...?! But Dai, deeply cynical, often taciturn, told me in no uncertain terms to tell that part of my brain to shut up. He may have teased me now and again about 'going full Glastonbury', but now I knew that he, too, could see that I was onto something.

To avoid these off days, I had to learn to let things progress at their own pace; I couldn't rush myself, or force feelings and connections that didn't exist. I came to this realisation, of all places, in a hot tub.

It was during our Unhoneymoon (the wedding had to be cancelled and rearranged so many times for reasons outside our control that we ended up having the honeymoon first) in Somerset. We had rented a beautiful cottage alongside the West Somerset Railway. As a fledgling student of Druidry, newly enamoured by the natural world, I was delighted by the views of rolling hills into the distance, the crooked fruit trees showering the garden with blossom, the primroses, bluebells and coiled ferns that bordered the hedges. And yes, we had a hot tub, although since we'd brought our two-year-old Spud with us, chances to use it were rather limited.

I spent much of our ten days away reclining in the conservatory of the cottage whilst the Spud took his daily nap on my lap (I hear some people get to put their kids to bed for a nap. We... are not those people. Whilst sometimes this is frustrating, it does at least force me to stop rushing around, and write, or read, or nap, for an hour or so each day, which is not bad practice). I watched robins, blackbirds, finches and thrushes come and go. We were visited by families of rabbits, and the occasional mouse. I took to putting our crumbs out on the garden path, where our cohabitors could snaffle them.

Now that I was spending so much more time being aware of nature, a sense of frustration was beginning to develop. I'd noticed it at home, and it had followed me here. I was cross with my lack of knowledge. All right, I could recognise an oak tree or a sycamore, but I didn't know a birch from a beech, a lime from an aspen. I didn't know what flowers were wild natives, and which were invasive foreign species. I couldn't identify different birds by their song, nor could I tell a wren from a sparrow. I was starting to get this feeling that the land was talking to me in a language I couldn't yet understand.

At least I knew the remedy for this problem. It's not exactly hard to find guidebooks nowadays – I had hope that I could educate myself out of this mental rut. But in the meantime, this lack of knowledge – not just about nature, but also about Druidry; I was proceeding through my books one at a time, carrying out the prescribed exercises in the prescribed order, determined to properly internalize the lessons and not leap headlong without proper understanding – coupled with an abundance of enthusiasm, led to... oh, this is slightly embarrassing to describe... trying really, really hard to Be Druidic.

By golly, I was going to Observe Nature. And it would know it had been observed! I inflicted the intensity of my Observant Druidic Gaze upon every passing flower, finch and sea snail. Not a leaf, not a pebble was safe from the depths of my interest. That sense of connection I had so enjoyed wavered in the face of this ferocious cataloguing. It also got exhausting pretty fast. And, okay, maybe a little boring.

I ended up feeling quite fed up. The morning started out well with a stroll on the beach, but by naptime we were all snarking at each other. Despite my resolution to use this time away as an unofficial retreat, I had started using my mobile data to check my emails and take surveys, and in the afternoon, I even found myself back on that dratted Pinterest.

I started to feel that I was clinging too hard to some idea of 'being Druidly', and by trying to force a passion for paying attention to every blade of grass, I was losing that sense of connection to the whole. Not only that, but I was treading a little too close to the danger zone of play-acting a Wise, Nature-Loving Druid, before I'd even really come to understand what being a student of Druidry meant for me.

A little disillusioned, I began to miss the rush, the buzz of a big shopping trip. Camden, perhaps, or Selfridges, or the North Laines of lovely Brighton. Colour and cafes, shopping bags slung over my arm. Oh, I missed how good I used to feel about how I looked, when I was younger and slimmer and, well, less muddy... Never mind the expense, the time, the complete self-obsession, how it gradually began to detract from everything else, how I could never keep up that lifestyle as a full-time parent – I'd enjoyed it at the time, hadn't I?

Later on that day, Dai took the Spud out for a walk. Alone in the cottage, I quickly realised that it was time to pull myself together. Feeling slightly ridiculous, I went into the garden, obscured from the railway by tall, thick hedges, and put myself through a quick sun salutation. Then I took off my clothes and got into the hot tub, naked.

It was utter luxury. The sky was blue, the air warm, the light gilding the apple blossom with a peachy hue as the sun began its descent into the west. Immediately I felt less miserable, less conflicted, more buoyant.

The last time I'd skinny-dipped was in Topaz's mum's swimming pool, perhaps seven years ago. We'd been eating homemade whisky ice cream; the pool was ringed with tealights flickering in the dark. I rode, surreally and memorably, upon a giant rubber duck, shrieking with laughter. Back then, I was in the midst of recovery from disordered eating. Skinny dipping was a good laugh, for a start, but also a way to reconnect with my body, to see it as something other than an enemy.

The last time I'd been swimming was the previous year in Pembrokeshire, when Dai and the Spud were on a supply run for dinner. I hadn't shaved my legs in a week, and the soft water had played havoc with my skin, but I put my swimming costume on, grabbed a towel, walked across the road to the beach and plunged into the cold blue sea. I was freezing and unkempt and bone-tired, but I felt so free, so strong, half-wild and salt-mad, and so glad to be alive.

The hot tub may not have been tidal, but the water and fresh air put me back in my body and brought me home to myself. I felt renewed.

When later I settled myself on a bench in the garden, enjoying the sun on my face, and went to write in my journal about the day's experiences, I had to laugh when I noticed the date. It was May 14th – exactly two years since I had started this entire journey.

Chapter 10

Brigid

After the skinny dip that soothed my spirit, I decided to reroute myself back to the concept of authenticity. Of course I was still interested in Druidry – the profound experiences I had had were too big in my mind for me to be discouraged so easily. But I was going to ease up on myself a bit.

However, the following day was a difficult one. The Spud was deeply out of sorts – teething, and possibly homesick – and eventually threw an Oscar-worthy tantrum in a harbour-side gift shop that resulted in us immediately calling it a day and whisking him back to the cottage to try to settle him for his nap. Upon waking, he was still stroppy. I was tripped up and bitten in short succession, and became increasingly cross with Dai cloistering himself away with his tablet instead of being on hand, possibly with a whip and chair. At last I shoved my feet into my shoes and stormed out of the cottage.

I don't think that this tantrum of my own was all to do with the Spud and Dai. Partly, I was frustrated that even here in the middle of nowhere I was still plagued by overshopping and semi-obsessive thoughts about how I ought to dress. I was spending too much on things I didn't need again. Despite my good intentions, I hadn't managed to give myself a week off from emails and surveys, and occasionally – like most parents, I think – I felt like the world's worst mother, and rather as though I'd blundered into a life meant for someone else. Someone who was probably less selfish, more put together, less anxious, and definitely less prone to talking to trees.

I found a footpath signposted from the nearest village and set out across the fields feeling miserable and hopeless. It hadn't dawned on me yet that although we'd been to wildlife parks and cider farms and all manner of lovely and interesting places, I hadn't been taking my daily walks, which at home in the normal scheme of things I depended upon to keep myself on a fairly even keel. Without a coat or a phone, and with only 10p in my pocket, I was nevertheless in a foul enough mood that I entertained the idea of disappearing into the hills and never going back. I felt guilty for childishly walking out, ashamed of my short temper, but also trapped and lost and confused, and very alone.

Three vast, sloping fields, a flock of sheep and a winding, muddy lane later, I encountered a bemused shepherd. He was the quintessential Somerset country man – dressed all in dark earthy colours, wellies and flat cap, holes in his worn sweatshirt, round-faced and ruddy. He carried a wooden walking staff in one hand and held the rope leash of a tawny, patient dog in the other. He was happy to chat for a while, if amused by my muddied cork eco-trainers, men's jeans (better pockets) and lack of map or weather-appropriate clothing.

We spoke briefly about tourism, the weather, where exactly I was (I knew I wasn't lost, I knew how to find my way back to the cottage, but I also stood little hope of explaining to Dai exactly where I had been!). After this meeting I walked on a little further – through another gate, I crossed the railway line on a sweeping curve lined by trees and wildflowers, and found a beautiful green lane, like a tunnel of ivy and ferns and twisted trees. The rain had been heavy that week, and water was trickling down the middle of the path, over the stones, like a waterfall. It was gorgeous, and I would have loved to explore further, but it was also muddy, and getting on towards sunset. I'm no stranger to night walking, but wandering unknown, secluded places in the dark without a phone didn't seem like my brightest idea. Besides, I knew it wasn't fair to leave Dai and the crotchety Spud for too much longer.

As I trekked – all right, squelched – back across the fields, it dawned on me that I could treat the appearance of the shepherd and his deeply practical approach to personal grooming as an answer to the stupid questions about shopping and style that, even here, even now, continued to plague me. I could treat this meeting as though it were a sign, telling me – keep focusing on nature and the outdoors! Screw Pinterest; screw shopping-as-a-hobby. Get yourself some decent walking boots and throw yourself wholeheartedly into being this journal-writing, Druidry-studying, birdwatching person who loves to do yoga in the garden, watch the sunset, and occasionally swim naked. Stop focusing so much on the surface of everything. Feeling heartened by this sense, however imaginary, of having received guidance and direction, I went back to my family in a much better mood.

I was looking forward to Brighde's Blessing at Glastonbury Goddess House for my birthday, but as time hastened towards it, I was beginning to feel that my fascination with this multifaceted, ancient goddess was not the one-way street that I had assumed.

Starting not long before I made the booking at Goddess House, references to Brigid – or Bride, Brid, Brighid, Breed, Bridey, or her many other variant names – or her Christian counterpart Saint Brigit – began showing up repeatedly in material I was reading, both online and in book form.

At first, I didn't think anything of this. I read a lot around Paganism and Goddess spirituality, so the frequent presence of a well-known and popular goddess was hardly a surprise. Then Amazon started recommending me books about Brigid. Intrigued, I saved a couple to my wish list and carried on doing my thing.

Over the next few months, well, Brigid intensified. By this point I was noticing that I couldn't pick up a book, or open a blog or magazine without finding reference to Brigid.

I said jokingly to Dai, "I think a goddess is trying to get my attention." Quite understandably, he made a quip about straitjacket fittings – immediately I felt a bit daft, and somewhat defensive. But really, what would a deity be talking to me for? Even if there existed such a thing, which I wasn't sure I quite believed.

Still. There was a little spark burning inside me! Excitement? Hope? I remembered that, when I'd been scrolling the Goddess House treatment list, seeing the name 'Brighde' had stopped me in my tracks.

Two days later, a book – *Tending Brigid's Flame*[48] – arrived in the post, a gift from Dai.

That weekend, I picked up a fiction book in the back room of the charity shop where I work, and flicked through the pages; the name 'Sister Brighid' leaped out at me. I laughed out loud.

Later on that same day, Dai and I had an appointment to meet our first 'real Druid'. Lady Idril, Crone of Avebury, was the handfasting celebrant we had been put in touch with by the manager of our new wedding venue, and I was really excited to meet her and learn more about the ceremony.

We met at the pub, and I liked her straight away. She was short and ageless, with the air of a woman who would not suffer fools. Her bobbed hair was sleek and glossy crow-black, with a single beaded dreadlock snaking from beneath down to her waist. A flowing earth-brown dress, silver jewellery, no make-up.

She and Dai were soon swapping mead recipes. She had a wicked sense of humour and a wild, raucous laugh. I must admit to thinking once or twice of Terry Pratchett's whip-smart, irreverent, no-nonsense witches.

Eventually we got down to hammering out the details of the ceremony. One aspect that pleasantly surprised me was that we had the option to choose which Goddess and God would be called upon. Dai and I looked at each other across the wooden picnic bench.

"You know who I'm going to say," I told him.

"You're going to say Brigid," said Dai, and I nodded firmly, feeling no hesitation.

That night, I decided it was time to start researching Brigid. I'd been feeling confident about choosing to look deeper into Druidry, and I didn't want to get too attached – so to speak – to a goddess when I didn't know yet how she might fit within that framework. After all, I was trying to keep things simple for myself! I knew that some eclectic Pagans might choose to work with deities from radically different pantheons, but the connections I had made so far were first and foremost with the land – Greek or Egyptian deities didn't feel like a good fit with my inner landscape of cow parsley, flint and rolling chalk hills. Would an Irish goddess be more amenable? And what was I going to do, if not? I could hardly just ignore a deity tapping on my shoulder.

I hadn't really even made up my mind how I felt about the idea of a goddess, I grumbled inwardly as I typed 'Druid goddesses' into my Ecosia search bar (pro tip: Ecosia is like Google, except that for every 45 searches you make, they plant a tree). Did I even *believe* in deity?

My introduction to Goddess spirituality had been through a book my friend Alice gave me – Laurie Cabot's *Power of the Witch*.[49] It's a little dated now, and some of the historical research she cites has been strongly questioned, but reading her take on prehistoric Goddess worship and matrifocal cultures really made me feel differently about our current patriarchal society, and about myself as a woman, in a way no list of goddess attributes, names or correspondences ever had. For the first time, I understood the empowerment in connecting with a feminine deity. I *wanted* to believe; I just wasn't sure if I could make the leap into faith yet.

My search loaded, and I tapped the first link that came up, entitled 'List of Druid Gods and Goddesses'. And there she was – "Brigid – Goddess of fire, healing, motherhood, agriculture, inspiration, learning, divination, poetry, prophecy, the forge."[50] On the OBOD website, I was delighted to read, "[Brigid] is specifically a patroness to the Druids in her aspects of poetry (Bards), healing and prophecy (Ovate), and blacksmithing (Druids)."[51]

That little spark of hope inside me roared up into a bright flame. The signs and coincidences I had been following were coming together, forming a glorious constellation.

The following night, Dai and I were in bed reading on our tablets. "Do you believe me," I asked, absent-mindedly perusing this year's edition of an almanac on Amazon, trying to discern if next year's might be useful. "About all this Brigid stuff, I mean? You don't think I'm deluding myself?"

As I spoke, I clicked onto an image from a reader review. It was a map; I couldn't make out what of, so I zoomed in – then I went hot all over, my skin prickling. It was a map of a pilgrimage route around St Brigit's holy places in Ireland. I turned my tablet to show Dai, and we stared at each other for a moment before Dai said, "I think we'd better set up an altar to Brigid."

Not knowing what, exactly, to do with an attentive goddess, I searched online for Brigid's holy places, operating on the vague notion that since everything I'd experienced so far had been largely nature-based and connected to the physical world, a meditation or visualisation wasn't going to cut the mustard. A list[52] came up, and I started reading the locations out to Dai, feeling my awe and hope and terror growing stronger as I did so. It was like a list of places Dai and I had visited in recent years – not least our little cottage in Pembrokeshire, which was almost dead in the centre of an area called St Bride's Bay. Glastonbury Tor, where I was planning to visit for my thirtieth birthday, also has a strong Brigid connection – she is depicted in a carving on St Michael's Tower at the top of the Tor. I felt shaky, a little dizzy. Those last doubts of mine, about how 'real' this all was, were swept away.

Over the following months, I have begun regularly tending a flame in Brigid's name. Dai now enjoys looking out for Brigid references everywhere I go – like a sort of spiritual Where's Wally. I'd read stories from Pagans who had spectacular tales of how they encountered their patron God or Goddess, and had assumed it was just the sort of thing that happened to other people. It was hard to overcome that last kernel of cynicism, that little voice that kept saying, "You're being silly!", and eventually I became quite forthright about asking for signs that I wasn't deluded.

Some of these communications – I went to a Church of England school; it's fair to say that finding an appropriate way of speaking to an ancient Celtic goddess has been a learning curve – are too personal for me to disclose here, but suffice to say that I finally realised that I had a two-way channel open, and I could ask questions to which I would receive answers (when I was in the right frame of mind to perceive them). I don't mean, like, lo the clouds parted and the voice of Brigid spoke unto me. More like – as an example – a brief image in my mind's eye, giving information which later was confirmed in a book I picked up at random. Subtle things, which I might have dismissed had I not been learning to be open to them.

Not that it was all plain sailing and marvellous clairvoyance (I wish!). Starting to open my mind to communications from other-than-human beings was exciting and revelatory, but also kind of exhausting. I'd love to be able to wrap up the consumerism side of my story here by telling you that once I found Druidry – and Brigid – I never overshopped again and became a peaceful and mysterious magical bardic soothsayer, but nah. Turns out that trying to be super mystical and keep my antennae open for signs and portents and communications from all beings at all times was a bit overwhelming, and I found myself swinging back towards obsessive online browsing as a way to decompress and switch off.

Unsurprisingly, my spending took an upswing again. Not in a serious or harmful way, but enough to get my attention. I put myself back on a thirty-day shopping ban and stopped trying to find gods and spirits in every river and hedgerow.

However, now that we knew the significance of the name St Bride, Dai and I decided to treat our annual trip to St Bride's Bay a little differently. I've jokingly referred to the trip as a pilgrimage before, but this time it actually was. Although, it didn't quite go the way I expected.

I really did try not to get my hopes up, but in all honesty, having experienced such undeniable synchronicities for so many weeks I went prepared for a big spiritual experience.

On the first full day of our holiday, we drove to the village of St Bride's Bay itself and parked up outside the chapel. Defying the forecast, the weather was glorious, the sky vivid blue and swept with gossamer clouds. I had birdseed in my pockets to give to the land, and a Tupperware full of dried lavender from my garden, which I had made into bunches to give as offerings to Brigid when and where it seemed appropriate to do so.

As I walked ahead of my family through the small churchyard – looking out over the glimmering curve of the sea, such a perfect reflection of the sky that it was hard to tell where one ended and the other began – my heart was in my mouth as I waited to perceive something. A sign. A vision. A spiritual hand on my shoulder. But... nothing. And in the end, less than that – I had hoped, at the very least, to see the statue of St Bride in the chapel, the only statue in existence that depicts the Christian saint (who may or may not be, or represent, the much older goddess) holding a Druid's stang.

Except, the chapel was closed. And firmly locked. On a Sunday after COVID restrictions were at last lifted. I felt somewhat at a loss. And slightly disgruntled. But I left some seed for the birds anyway, and we went down to the beach.

It was unusually quiet for such a beautiful tourist hotspot on a sunny weekend, and we decided to paddle in the water. Though I felt a bit confused – had I been misguided, to seek a Pagan goddess in the chapel of a Christian saint? – the sheer visual deliciousness of the bay did much to lift my spirits. I took some time by myself to walk along the cliffs, enjoying the wildflowers and the lush green ferns, and found a quiet and secluded spot overlooking the beach where I spoke, quietly, to Brigid. As the greenery hummed with crickets, I had a sense that something there, something in or of the land, was laughing at me. I don't have the Sight – and having read Morgan Daimler's books on the Fair Folk[53] I know what's out of my depth to go dabbling in – but my best guess for this feeling of amusement and mischief was that perhaps the Good Neighbours were around, so I laid down one of my lavender bundles, politely gabbled something well-intentioned about peace and friendship, and decided to mosey back down to the beach.

On my way, I cheekily asked for a sign that my offering had been well-received, and took it as a positive indicator when a small blue butterfly appeared moments later. Was this really a sign? I have no idea. I'm not sure at what point 'being attuned to subtle communication' becomes 'seeing what you want to see'. But on this occasion, I decided to feel grateful for the butterfly and go play on the beach with my son.

Later, knee-deep in the surf, the thought arose in my mind: "You're looking in the wrong place."

Once more that week we set out in search of the goddess. We drove to St Non's Chapel, which we had visited the year before. I had been particularly taken with St Non's Well, a natural spring which allegedly sprung up as Non gave birth to David (Patron Saint of Wales, kind of a big deal in these parts) during a thunderstorm. The well itself is beautiful, set on an expanse of rolling cliffs, surrounded by flowering gorse and tiger lilies, and overlooked by a serene statue of St Non, draped in flowers and jewellery and other offerings.

Again there was no one else around when we arrived, and I stripped down to my undies and lowered myself gingerly into the clear, very cold water of the well.

The link between St Non and St Bride, or St Brigit, is slightly vague. There is a stained-glass window in St Non's Chapel, a fairly modern building, which depicts St Bride, and historian Monica Sjoo has posited that the spring was there before Non and the birth of David, possibly already a sacred place where a priesshood may have resided.[54]

Brigid or no Brigid, having immersed myself in the sacred well, it seemed fitting to leave another of my lavender offerings here. In the side of the well there is a niche – conveniently only visible if one happens to be in the water – and I tucked my bunch of lavender there.

I scrambled back into my jeans safe in the knowledge that I'd soon dry out, feeling the icy water in the small of my back as we made our way up the cliff path towards the chapel. The chapel, which lies in the grounds of a retreat centre, was built from stones found locally, and there was a sign propped up in the doorway asking visitors to leave the door open for the swifts nesting in the roof. It was a charming place and certainly very special in its own right. I was interested to see that the windowsill before the stained-glass window showing St Bride bore a large collection of offerings and oddments, gifts of all kinds, from toys and keyrings to seashells, photographs and handwritten prayers. But I still didn't feel like I'd got what I was looking for.

As we headed back to the car, I looked out over the vast greenness of Wales, the Preseli hills visible in the far distance, and I felt... something. Amusement. Impatience. The more I looked at the land, the more I found myself thinking, "*There* you are."

I *had* been looking in the wrong place. Brigid, it seemed, was telling me that she was not to be found in church nor in any chapel, at least not by me. Brigid, I perhaps should note, is not generally thought of as an earth goddess, but she is certainly a British one (the name 'Britain' itself comes from one of Brigid's older names, and we see her as Britannia on the fifty pence coin even today[55]). The message, I felt, was that once again, it was time for me to turn my attention back to the land, the earth, the ground under my feet.

Chapter 11

The Good Neighbours

An unexpected but not unwelcome side effect of the Pembrokeshire pilgrimage was a resurgence in my interest in environmentalism. Rearranging our wedding multiple times and attempting to facilitate a house move, whilst Dai seemed to be working every hour under the sun, had induced a state something like burnout. I was sharing the petitions and monitoring my energy usage, as ever, but it was something that had become rote – a duty, a chore. I was too tired and stressed out to put any real passion into it.

Besides the obvious benefits of being able to spend restful time in a tranquil place, the astonishing beauty of the Welsh coastline reminded me of what it was I loved so much about the earth and the small part of it on which I am lucky enough to dwell. As we watched the moon rise and the tide come sweeping in to an unspoilt, almost hidden bay, the water clear as glass, it seemed unthinkable, almost blasphemous, that mankind would pollute this, would despoil this, in the endless quest for progress and ever more consumption.

Perhaps there were Fair Folk amongst the foxgloves and heather of the cliffs. Perhaps the wells and springs in the hills were sacred or even magical. Perhaps the land itself might be conscious, self-aware, sovereign. I believed it; I wanted to believe it. But I also understood that in some ways it should make no difference – we should protect the land and cherish it not because we are pagan but because we are human.

Humanity has become synonymous with destruction and decimation. But we, like any other beast or being, are also part of this biosphere. We seem to have forgotten how to give as well as take. We have forgotten how to enjoy the world, to luxuriate in beauty and sensation, our senses dulled by the overstimulation of our pinging devices and mechanical toys.

I suspect it's no coincidence that in this particularly spectacular corner of Britain I saw a great flourishing of the sustainability movement – from climate change protest art to foraging courses and wild food cafes.

Shortly before this holiday, we'd moved house, leaving behind our beige rental with a sigh of relief and proceeding to spend a fraught weekend with a bevy of exceedingly kind friends helping us squish our possessions into a 1940s two-up, two-down.

We'd been able to snare the place for a good price due to its general state of mild dilapidation. There was no gas safety certificate, the back door fell off in my hand a week or so after we moved in, there were mushrooms growing in the conservatory, and Topaz found a spoon, a needle, and a glass vial containing a brown substance hidden on top of the kitchen cupboards. But the garden was large (albeit consisting entirely of weeds, mud and broken glass) and the location was good. Raised by a self-described anarchist, I was suspicious of the idea of a mortgage (isn't it just renting from the bank?) but our vague long-term plan was to renovate the place and make it homely, sell it on and look for a smallholding in Wales, preferably not too far from the sea. Well, I can dream, can't I?

With Dai working long hours the unpacking and renovations were frustratingly slow. Caring for the Spud full-time limited what I could get done, and it wasn't long before I gave up on paint samples and the chaos of boxes and turned my attention to the garden.

Living in a much more urban area – close to the centre of town – was a steep learning curve for me. I didn't miss our rental, but I really missed the nature reserve, and having the river practically on our back doorstep. The scrubby, defiant urban weeds and council-manicured parks and cemeteries which I could now access seemed a poor substitute, and I felt the richness and vitality of the connection with nature that had become something like sustenance for my soul dwindling into a vague background noise, and sometimes not even that.

I flung myself into yard work with a desperation somewhat akin to fury. Our daily walks, the lifeblood of my relationship with the environment but also with my son, were replaced by ferocious digging, as I fought to grow a lawn from seed before muddy toddler footprints turned the entire downstairs of our house into a swamp. In my spare time I went hard into my reading on polytheism, Heathenry, Druidry, traditional witchcraft and Wicca, trying to recapture that spark of genuine enchantment I had felt. Likewise, I found my dress sense tending more towards elaborate eyeliner and mystical jewellery, as I strove to find some kind of magic in everyday living.

Luckily, this tendency to drift into style-over-substance was fairly short-lived. Once I realised that the repetitive work of endlessly digging didn't result in the same sense of rootedness of walking around an area, day-in, day-out, I took a deep breath and stopped trying to create a perfect garden in a single summer. The lawn was scraggly but it was there. The mulch was down where I wanted the veg patch to be. My potted herbs were flourishing. It would do – time to turn my focus outwards again.

The Spud was relieved to be back on our daily jaunts. We followed the river through patchy urban woodland and under graffitied bridges. We picked blackberries in the cemetery and watched trains come thundering past the nature reserve. Soon I realised that my 'mystical uniform' made me feel self-conscious and attracted more attention than I wanted when I was creeping under bridges and wandering through alleys, and slipped back into my boring, practical, useful, liberating jeans.

I began to look for other ways that I could connect to this new area and be of service to the community. I started frequenting the Saturday market to buy our bread and other staples; when I needed garden plants, Dai and I headed to the local nursery instead of a big chain store (and were pleasantly surprised by how excellent it was). When I saw that a local paper was looking for volunteer writers, I signed up to write about environmental issues. And I went back to charity shop work on the weekends – a risky move for a shopaholic, but I'm pleased to say that I managed to keep myself in check!

However, being situated closer to town certainly didn't help my consumerist tendencies in general. For the first few weeks in the new house we had no net curtains or blinds downstairs, and I felt constantly like I was being watched – probably because I was. An open, lighted window has an almost irresistible pull for many people, after all – it's human nature to be curious about how others live. We were also situated on a main thoroughfare, so I was now seeing far more people on a daily basis than I ever had before, and, perhaps more importantly to that fashion-loving part of my brain, they were seeing me. For a while I felt compelled to present myself as if I were walking out onto a stage each day – I was preoccupied by how well each outfit 'expressed' me, and my browsing for new outfits suddenly intensified.

There were other, more practical facets to consider as well – it was simply easier, now, to get a pizza delivered if the little one was asleep in my lap, rather than wake him up to cook. It was easier to pop down to the Nepalese takeaway to try momo, or grab a pre-packaged picnic whilst we were on the go. And of course, we now had a house to renovate and decorate. For my garden work I was trying to reuse a lot of what I found kicking around the property – old sinks became planters; gates became trellises. But indoors I found myself buying fripperies like candle holders and fairy lights on a disturbingly regular basis, until I realised the effect it was beginning to have on my wallet, and put myself back on a strict shopping ban.

I once thought that stopping overshopping would be as simple as just deciding not to buy stuff anymore. But it really hasn't been that simple. Over and over again I have had to look baldly at my spending behaviour, adjust, recalibrate, dust myself off and try again. Druidry helped – it gave me a lens to see the world through that was not so anthropocentric – but it didn't do miracles.

Over the years I'd come across a lot of spiritual and Pagan type books encouraging a mindset of abundance, of presenting the cosmos with one's shopping list, be it through spells and charms or manifestation – outside of Eastern traditions, I hadn't come across much in the way of praise for simplicity or restraint. It was only now that this started to seem odd to me, for a group of faiths and paths emphasising care for the earth and connection with nature.

I found myself turned off by witchcraft books with spells written out like recipes with lists of ingredients or trappings. I got irritated when I noticed that one well-known Pagan supply store was selling their herb-growing kits with pellets of peat (peat used in compost usually comes from peat bogs – the UK's peatlands are rare and drastically endangered ecosystems). (There are, happily, plenty of Pagan writers with a more ecological bent, as I discovered when I started looking with this in mind – please see the Further Reading section at the back of the book.) I started looking deeper into more than just Druidry – now I was reading about permaculture and organic gardening, zero waste kitchens and worm composting. I wasn't feeling that electric, goosebumps-raising sense of communication with something Other, but I was determined to do right by my own little patch of land. And stop buying quite so many candle holders.

However, returning to our new home after our trip to Wales, we soon came to discover that I might not have been feeling so connected to this urban environment, but it was certainly not going to let me ignore it either.

It started with our cutlery drawer. All our knives disappeared, overnight.

Then my left boot vanished. (This still has not made its way back from wherever it has gone to, but I live in hope.)

Then I started finding items of Dai's laundry when I was pruning the trees that had gone wild at the bottom of our garden, forlorn-looking socks threaded high up through the branches.

Then we lost power, inexplicably, for three hours – much to the bewilderment of the energy company.

One night at dinner, Dai and I held a conference about these mysterious events. Dai suggested that we perhaps ought to leave out offerings for the household spirits and Fair Folk. I felt a jolt of surprise and delight – okay, having no knives suddenly was a touch unhelpful, but here was the unexplained, showing up in our lives again when I hadn't been looking for it or straining to create it.

Dai pointed out that we had tidied the house and garden, set up nice altars, put offerings out for Lughnasadh – and then disappeared to Pembrokeshire without warning. Perhaps we had been rude!

Sure enough, a few bowls of milk later, our knives reappeared, and I stopped finding Dai's undergarments in the hedgerows. You can believe I was extremely trepidatious when I had to prune the three elder trees that had tangled together in the far corner of the garden – I apologised profusely before and after, and told them the entire time I was only trying to help! (Yes, I suspect the human neighbours think we are strange...)

Dai also had an unexplained encounter at this time, when he was out working late one night in his then job as a roadside recovery driver and mechanic. He says that it was a clear, still night, and he was on a hilltop with good visibility in all directions. He was changing the wheel on a Range Rover when something unseen passed over his shoulder and by his face at great speed, with a sound that he described as the rushing of many wings, "like a flock of starlings".

Dai, it should perhaps be noted, despite his general air of

cynicism and deeply practical nature, is actually far more sensitive to energies and – how can I put this? – non-traditionally-embodied entities than I am, having previously – for example – practised hands-on healing, and regularly encounters ghosts and spirits in old buildings and on the job. In fact, he can occasionally be found to have wandered into the cemetery on his way back from the pub and picked up a conversation (or an argument – in his words, "they started it") with the residents.

I, however, have no Sight-with-a-capital-S, and often in all honesty feel a bit lacking when I read books by the likes of Morgan Daimler and Emma Restall Orr, who have been conversant from childhood with beings I have never been able to vaguely perceive (except on that one memorable occasion with my friend Alec). What's the use, I have wondered, of me meddling blindfolded around the edges of the Otherworld?

Yet these experiences felt to me as though with our offerings – our acknowledgement, however inept – we had opened a door, even if only a chink. It was enthralling and wondrous, and sometimes a little scary – such as when I was sitting in the garden on a hot sleepless night, and heard two voices – speaking a language I didn't recognise, with a timbre like the crackling of dead leaves, which I don't believe could have been produced by any human throat – coming from the hedgerow at the bottom of the garden, backing onto the cemetery, accompanied by such a weighty sense of *presence* that I quietly got to my knees on the dusty grass until I felt calm enough to scurry back indoors.

My life was changing. I found myself creeping around at strange hours with dried herbs and bowls of milk and honey, possibly a bit wild-eyed and tangle-haired, smelling of incense and with dirty feet. And I loved it.

On a more materialistic note, around this time, I had a look at what I had been spending since 2019, when I first started my non-shopping challenge. I found that my spending on clothes had decreased by half, and my spend on books by approximately seventy-five per cent. Granted, I was still spending more than I wanted, but as I learned to make better choices and to source items second-hand, I was also seeing more improvements.

In fact, I put myself back on a thirty-day shopping ban as my birthday began to approach. Not because my spending was out of control, but because I wanted to give myself a break from those familiar, repetitive thoughts that surround shopping – the endless decisions and choices about what to buy or not to buy, what this or that item would express about me, whether supporting artisans and small indie businesses or buying second-hand was the more ethical choice, whether being ethical or eco-friendly was more important... I just felt I wanted my headspace back for a little while, so that I could concentrate more on other things. So that I could approach this milestone birthday with peace and clarity, or at least a reasonable facsimile thereof.

My attempt at a low-buy year had not gone overly well. There were two or three months when I managed a single 'frivolous' monthly purchase, but after that I fell off the wagon once again, and took several weeks to get myself back on an even keel. I had found that planning even a single purchase encouraged me to spend much more time browsing, both online and off, and focusing more on all those things I didn't yet have but might want. I ended up with a long list of things I wanted to buy throughout the year, and became unduly concerned that those things might be discontinued or sold out. A low-buy had seemed like a sensible, moderate option, but for me it wasn't the answer.

So it was much to my astonishment that those thirty days without shopping passed with little difficulty or struggle. Admittedly I had two or three false starts, where I remembered 'one last thing' I could really do with buying, but week one wasn't the gritted-teeth fiasco of stress and despair I remembered from those early days of 2019. Actually, it was... kind of easy? Even when a rainstorm drove the Spud and I to take shelter in B&M,

I really didn't want to buy anything. The relentless striving for novelty seemed to cease as soon as I gave myself permission to take a step back from it.

Which raised the question, why had I been shopping so much over the past few months? Habit? Boredom? That old chestnut, the Diderot effect?[56] It seemed that buying more only facilitated an endless cycle of wanting to buy still more.

In the second week I decided to take a break from endless Googling (or rather, Ecosia-ing), reading blogs, browsing the Kindle store and otherwise constantly seeking out new information. Instead I decided to put my focus into actually studying some of the books I had amassed at home (who else buys assorted self-help books, how-tos, guided meditations etc. and then never actually gets around to doing the exercises or following the steps? It's not just me, right?) and developing my personal gnosis (such as it is at this early stage!). This turned out to be quite beneficial in terms of concentration and actually getting things done, but incredibly difficult to put into practise – and still a work in progress.

I had one last push at a big clear-out. I'd been clinging to a lot of things that I didn't really wear out of what I can only describe as eco-anxiety, my head ringing with the adage 'the most sustainable item is the one you already own'. I'd recently read Bea Johnson's *Zero Waste Home*,[57] and found much wisdom in her advice that you can reduce your consumption by reducing your needs – and by this stage of the game I could see that I no longer needed a huge wardrobe.

This was not an easy process, but also not the battle it has been on previous occasions. I still couldn't put a neat and tidy label on 'my style', but I had a much better idea of what I liked to wear, and even better, what I would be excited to put on in the mornings. I was feeling more like myself – my true self – than I had in years. I was no longer obsessed with my appearance, but I had also at last given up the sackcloth and ashes.

I had come to understand that, although personal choices are important – and yes, all our lives will undergo changes as we adapt to a changing climate – my decisions would not singlehandedly doom or save the planet, and I learned to lighten up on myself a little bit. I'd discovered individuals like the artist Corinne Loperfido,[58] who lives as sustainably as she can – but still has a powerful and creative personal style.

However, I soon found that it wasn't going to be as simple as just chucking stuff into bags and sending it off for resale. Instead I ended up with a long-winded system whereby each day I chose an item from my pile of would-be discards, and tried to incorporate it into an outfit I actually liked and felt happy wearing. I was surprised to find that in the end, I didn't get rid of much, and I was able to wear and make use of a much greater proportion of my wardrobe. I even went so far as to dye some 'unwearables' and make them into something new, and with a bit of haphazard cutting and sewing turned some of my old oversized band tees into summery tank tops.

Again, the message was rammed home to me that I really didn't need to keep buying more things. I only needed to better appreciate the things that I already had.

By the end of this thirty-day mini-ban, I found that the biggest lesson I had learned from it was that I really needed to slow down. I was reading hurriedly and voraciously, trying to tick books off my list and level up my knowledge but at the expense of enjoyment; frantically attacking the garden during daylight hours, and I'd all but stopped scratch cooking and had fallen back on convenience foods. Annoyingly, I'd noticed I was also spending a lot of time fiddling about on my tablet to no real purpose, and watching the clock rather than engaging fully with whatever I was doing.

I was rushing from one thing to another around the house, cutting back on sleep to fit in more reading and research, and my meditation, exercise, writing, and other aspects of my spiritual life were forever being pushed onto the list of things to do 'later' – once I'd knocked the next important book off my To Be Read pile, or unpacked some more boxes, or rearranged the shelving in the shed. I even hurt my back whilst doing some DIY jobs I really should have waited for Dai to help me with, and ended up spending a weekend barely able to move, creaking around the house snarling at everyone.

It was definitely time for me to take a breather, get mindful, and reassess my priorities. I'd learned to control my overshopping – now I had to take a good look at how I wanted to fill that time instead, instead of constantly racing against the clock.

Hearteningly, I was also seeing changes in my community that showed an encouraging awareness of the benefits of reducing consumption – from both a financial and an environmental standpoint. The free prom dress rental shop, stocked with donated dresses, was reopening in a new venue post-COVID, and a new monthly clothing exchange was flourishing on the high street. We visited this once, and for the hardly princely sum of £3 to fill a carrier bag, were able to stock up the next two sizes of the Spud's wardrobe.

On the downside, it wasn't all good news. Having taken the train up to London to spend a day taking part in Extinction Rebellion's Impossible Rebellion protests, I came back on a bit of a high, feeling zeitgeisty and full of hope that maybe – just maybe – real change could be at hand, preferably in time to save something approaching the world as we know it. Yet the very next day, I was putting some rubbish in my mum's wheelie bin when I discovered that the people in the downstairs flat, who were moving out, had used her bin to dispose of fifteen or so handbags and several purses, many of which were leather, some of which were unused; a bunch of wrapping paper – still in its plastic shrink-wrap – and a lot of other perfectly reusable miscellanea, like boxes of unused Christmas cards and fancy gift bags. Our black bin collection locally, by the way, goes to the incinerator.

I rescued as much as I could carry, and rehomed the lot. Going through dustbins is not my idea of a fun time, and I cringe slightly writing this (the joys of potentially becoming 'that weird lass who believes in faeries and rummages in people's bins') but I couldn't in good conscience see brand new items sent to be incinerated.

It was a bit of a shock to the system to be so emphatically reminded that for many people – the majority of people – in our civilised society here in the global North, the planet and our ecosystem still does not come first, and maybe isn't even an afterthought.

Chapter 12

#Blessed

At last my thirtieth birthday rolled around. I had been trying not to let my expectations get out of hand as the day approached, but given all our recent experiences it was difficult not to anticipate prophetic visions or something of a similar spiritually-majestic ilk.

We rolled into Glastonbury on a sunny September afternoon, the day before my birthday, pirate shanties blaring from the car stereo. I was fizzing with excitement, but also horribly nervous as Dai and the Spud walked me to the doors of Goddess House and kissed me goodbye.

Inside the cool, quiet hallway of the House I slipped off my shoes as instructed and padded – barefoot and trying to seem totally nonchalant about it – into a large room where I could take a seat and fill in my consultation form. My therapist Natalia (as with most individuals in this book, I have changed her name for privacy) was an apparently ageless woman with silky black hair, prayer beads, and a trace of an accent.

When she left to prepare the therapy room, I put the pen down on the clipboard and took a moment to gather myself. My nerves were not due to any metaphysical reasons – I wasn't expecting the goddess herself to drop in and say hi – but purely the anxiety around not knowing what exactly to expect, and the possibility of stripping down to my knickers in front of a stranger.

As I sat and tried to convince myself that a professional holistic therapist operating in Glastonbury would have seen much stranger things than my nearly-naked flesh, I suddenly realised that there was an abundance of snowdrop and swan decorations in the room I was in – both symbols of Brigid. Then I noticed a Brigid's Cross in the hearth and the art on the walls – nearly opposite me was a painting of the goddess looking down at me, her eyes laughing, her lips curved with the trace of a smile.

I had to grin myself. I'd been settled to wait in the Brighde Room. How very appropriate.

Natalia ushered me up the stairs, both of us barefoot. The hush was palpable; the huge house sat silently on its foundations as if reverent. The afternoon sunshine slid softly through the tall windows and settled on the carpeted stairs.

Natalia led me into the Artha Treatment Room and we took seats facing each other. I clutched my backpack in my lap like an anxious schoolgirl as we went through all the preliminary chat and discussed what would happen during the treatment, then Natalia said, "Can I ask what made you decide to have this particular treatment?"

My face went hot. I hadn't ever discussed my interest in Brigid with anyone but Dai, and although this was the *Goddess* House, connected with the *Goddess Temple*, a lifetime's worth of not wanting to seem silly, gullible or foolish made me uncertain of my own perceptions, let alone my words.

"I hope you won't think I'm crazy," I mumbled, "but I've been feeling really drawn to Brighde – or Brigid – for a while now."

Natalia shook her head. "That's not crazy."

She was so calm and non-judgmental – pretty much what you'd expect from someone working in a building dedicated to the Goddess – that I found myself telling her most of the story – the synchronicities, the communications, the series of coincidences that seemed anything but coincidental. She listened patiently, nodding as though my babbling made perfect sense.

"It happened to me too," she said, when I eventually paused for breath. "Except for me it was swans. You know they are a symbol of her, one of her sacred creatures? When I first got interested in Brigid, I started seeing pictures of swans everywhere I looked, everywhere I went."

Looking down through the hole in the massage table, my eyes came to rest on a large chunk of quartz crystal, and then drifted closed. Gentle music filled the room. It was a hot day, and I was warm and comfortable under my protective layers of towels.

I listened with interest as Natalia addressed the Goddess Brigid and invited her to attend. Being Facebook-averse and fairly quiet about my Pagan leanings (until now, I guess) I'd never found or contacted any local Pagans or polytheists, so this was my first time hearing someone else addressing a goddess. I felt the hairs prickle on my arms and the nape of my neck.

Are you here, Brigid? I found myself asking, frustrated – not for the first or last time – with my limited senses, my inability to perceive.

Natalia continued praying softly, her hands resting lightly on my shoulders. She asked Brigid to bless me, and although I knew that this was part of the treatment, I remember feeling slightly awkward – did Natalia think I was worthy to receive such a blessing? Did she mind interceding on my behalf, when I was a total stranger? I suspect that this was largely a reflection of the self-doubt I had felt when Brigid first began to make herself known to me, and I have to imagine that Natalia, as a consummate professional healer and Priestess, was making no such judgements about me one way or another! Any thoughts about being undeserving were purely down to me – I was quite surprised by my negative self-perception.

I had a great deal of difficulty in relaxing and 'switching off'. My keenness to experience something profound or magical was working against me, and despite being in such a woman-centred space and no stranger to spa treatments, I felt uncommonly shy and vulnerable in my state of undress. The only thing out of the ordinary I experienced was a faint sense of gentle, tingling warmth from Natalia's hands up my legs as she performed an energetic healing.

Near the end of the session, Natalia invoked the elements to bring balance to my body, and spoke further blessings for my new decade. This was exactly the kind of symbolic marker I had hoped for, for my thirtieth birthday, and I was surprised to find myself tearing up a little. I still felt that small shameful sense of being silly or in some way unworthy, but I did my best to let the words sink in to me.

"Thank you," I said afterwards. "That was beautiful."

"Thank *you*," Natalia said. "I liked working with you. You have a good energy." I was rather pleased with that! "You're very tense, though. I'd suggest doing some yoga, or dance maybe. Something that moves the whole body. Even your legs are tense," she added, rather worriedly.

When Natalia left me to sip a cool glass of water and get dressed, I stayed reclining another few moments, thinking. I had expected – perhaps I should say 'hoped' – to feel different after my healing. A symbolic shedding of the previous decade's woes, like a snakeskin. But here I was, still me. Overthinking, awkward, tense.

I sat up on the bench, pushed my hair out of my eyes, and smiled at myself in the mirror. Without my glasses, by candlelight and sunlight, my reflection was softened, gilded. I looked like someone I could love.

"Thank you," I said quietly to Brigid.

Because I was still me. I would always be me. I had changed my body, my hair, my face, my clothes, time and time again, and guess what? It was always going to be just me underneath. I couldn't magic it away or buy myself a new heart and soul. So, it was time to learn to like it.

On top of my pile of clothes was an 'inspiration' card. By accident or design I don't know – I could have asked Natalia about it, but I didn't. It read, "Seek the quiet and replenish your energy,", which I figured was pretty good advice, and then underneath, the single word, "*Oak*". This made me laugh out loud – St Brigit's church in Ireland was built beneath a huge, ancient and possibly sacred oak tree, hence the name Kildare – from Cill-Dara, 'Church of the Oak'. I tucked it into my pocket (and when I pulled it out over takeaway chips and blackberry mead to read to Dai, sitting on a picnic bench outside our accommodation that night, he burst out laughing too. I must have looked at him somewhat quizzically, because he just pointed upwards – we were sitting under a young oak).

I left Goddess House with my battered backpack slung over my shoulder, blinking in the golden light of late afternoon. Glastonbury high street was as madcap as usual, and I realised as I set off with no particular destination that I actually felt rather drunk. Since I hadn't yet touched a tipple that day, I can only surmise that this giggly, spacey, lightheaded feeling was something to do with Natalia's energetic healing. I floated alongside the road like a balloon on a string, feeling cheerful but also slightly raw and exposed. For a while I wandered the shops, and I'm pleased to say that even in this slightly altered state, I made only one purchase, a book. By the time I met up with Dai and the Spud I had come back down to earth, but I was certainly glad to tuck into some dinner and ground myself.

The next morning – my thirtieth birthday – I awoke to brilliant sunshine streaming between the curtains of our rented accommodation – a studio apartment in the renovated outbuilding of a small farm just outside Glastonbury. The three of us were outside whilst the grass was still wet with dew, feeding the chickens, exploring the small orchard, wandering through the meadow down to the stream, which was so abundant with trout that Dai suggested it was almost possible to walk from one side to the other without getting wet feet.

We set off early for the Tor, hoping to reach the summit before the heat of the day reached its peak. It was a glorious day for the walk. Sadly, the White Spring temple at the foot of the Tor was still closed following COVID; I had hoped to visit the shrine to

Brigid that lies within, but on this occasion, it was not to be.

The Tor stands high over the town, an imposing but beautiful sentinel, visible and unmistakable for miles around. We parked our car on its flank with several others – even this early on a Sunday morning – and set off up the footpath. Despite the 'no camping' signs there were a handful of tents scattered around the base of the hill, with clothing hanging from the trees, a scruffy brown-and-white dog sniffing joyously in the long meadow grass, and a barefoot, bearded man playing a didgeridoo. I watched him for a while, feeling the faint sense of envy I often feel when presented with lifestyles well outside of the mainstream.

"I wonder what his life is like," I mused to Dai, already mentally fitting our belongings into a VW camper van.

Dai is not one to get caught up in my romantic fantasies. "Cold," he pronounced. "And smelly."

As the ground sloped upwards beneath our feet, I was buzzing with anticipation – I had read plenty about the special, sacred energies of the Tor. But I was also keeping myself in check – so far, nothing in this journey had gone quite the way I expected.

And in the event, I was glad for that attitude. We toiled our way up the steep side of the hill, past orchards and grazing sheep, up the narrow and winding stair to the summit. The expanse of Somerset fell away all around us, a vast and uninterrupted vista on this day of clear blue skies. The tower rose in the centre, solid and inscrutable, a gateway to nowhere. The scene was set for me to step into my next decade.

The Spud gambolled on the grass, between tourist types in serious walking gear, and a few long-haired, earnest young men holding bodhrans. Dai kept close to stop him diving over the edge.

And me? I was plastered nearly flat on the grass, well away from any sheer edges, hyperventilating.

Somehow, in the midst of all the excitement, I hadn't taken into consideration my crippling fear of heights. Eventually I was able to give the tower a cursory investigation, but when Brigid didn't immediately leap out at me, I sought Dai. "This is lovely and all, but can we get down now?" I pleaded.

Luckily, I was aided and abetted in my deep and abiding desire to return to flat ground by the Spud, who, with remarkable accuracy, had pinpointed an ice cream van parked down below and was demanding sugary sustenance forthwith. He and Dai set off at the double, and with great relief I gingerly made my way down behind them. So I'm sorry to say that, if there were any mystical energies at work on the Tor, I was in no state to notice them, and as a symbolic step into my next decade, the whole debacle was a rather anticlimactic one.

Still, as I slipped off my sandals to grip the ground better, and made my way to join my partner and son beside the ice cream van – Didgeridoo Man still doing his thing in the background – I was pleased that I'd done it, and feeling pretty good.

Looking back now over the last few years, I can say that the decision to stop shopping, and bring to an end my unremitting cycle of buy-dispose-and-buy-again, was without doubt one of the best choices I have ever made.

At the beginning, I thought that quitting shopping would be a sacrifice, but I have gained so much more than I have given up. Choosing to cut my consumption has liberated me from the feeling of not being enough; it has enabled me to build deeper relationships with my human community; it has introduced me to new ways of relating to and connecting with nature and the land, and the spirits and deities that are part of that whole. It has helped me to be more creative, more self-reliant, more confident, more responsible, more compassionate and more capable. If you think I am overstating the benefits, then by all means, try it for yourself.

Looking harder at my purchasing behaviours also encouraged me to look more closely at what, exactly, I was purchasing. We have talked about sweatshop-made clothes, which are often poor quality and designed to be disposable. I have also made changes within my home; from the products I clean with – from a Druidic perspective it's hard to justify using chemicals that are damaging to the environment once released into the air or rinsed down the drain – to what we eat and what 'disposable' products and packaging we are willing to use and accept. Granted, this is neither quick nor easy, and will most likely remain a work in progress for some time, but it also feels very necessary.

One area where I was able to make a lot of change with relative ease was my purchasing of cosmetics. I no longer wear make-up regularly as I don't wish to depend on the application of a product to feel good about myself, but I still have to clean myself, I use a fair amount of skincare products and I enjoy perfume. I was horrified when I started looking further into what goes into many of these products[59] – from a personal and an ecological standpoint – and I now only use natural, cruelty-free products with minimal ingredients, and I buy a lot less, and less often. Generally speaking, if I wouldn't eat it, I don't put it on my face either. A side-effect of this is that the Spud no longer seems to suffer from eczema, so that's a win.

Body image is another area where I have benefited from shopping less. Reduced exposure to advertising and social media has reduced my tendencies to compare myself to others, and to feel dissatisfied with who I am and how I look. Obviously, I'm human, so I have good days and bad days, but overall I feel much more grounded and surer of myself than I did throughout my twenties. The gremlin on my shoulder has largely been silenced – with a little help from intuitive eating,[60] a bit of growing up, and a large dose of self-acceptance. I've learned that I can't shop my way to being someone else, and at last I can say that I wouldn't want to do that anyway. Like it or not, this is me.

Of course, one of the biggest and most unexpected changes to my life since I cut back my consumption has been my discovery of Druidry, which has given me a framework for making further changes to my attitude and lifestyle. It seems that the more I learn on this path, the more there is that I don't know, which is so exciting. 'There is more to heaven and earth, Horatio,' so to speak.

Some of the concepts intrinsic to Druidry, such as care for the earth and being of service, have been incredibly helpful in bolstering my commitment to becoming less consumerist, and have also made my life more meaningful, bringing real understanding that I may just be one individual, but I am a part of a community, a landscape, a biosphere. Nothing that we do stands alone – everything creates an effect, be it good or bad, and having awareness of this has made it all the more important to me to 'be the change I want to see in the world'.

Even on a basic level, eating the food we grow in the garden strengthens my relationship with the land,[61] and although even children know that seeds planted in the ground become vegetables, trees and flowers, it's quite amazing to me how satisfying this is, and how much delight I get from eating something I have planted. Honestly, I recently became quite emotional over a beetroot risotto.

I also have found immense value in the concept of the Bardic grade. Imagination and creativity is so often stifled and quashed in our society unless it can turn a profit, or fit into a grid of squares and sell an image, a lifestyle, a brand, a product. To know that there are those still holding space in the world for the storytellers, the poets, the dancers, the artists, performers, writers, musicians and wandering mythmakers of all stripes makes me believe there might still be hope for us as a species yet. It no longer feels silly or odd to play a little tune for the Good Folk. In fact it might be one of the most meaningful things that I do.

Now that I am looking, properly, I see this in my friends and family – the value of creativity. Very often, we are most alive when we are creating, but creativity does not always look the way we are taught to expect. I see the spark of inspiration, the 'fire in the head' of poetry and myth, in Topaz when she runs a game of D&D as Dungeon Master, as she weaves a story and carries us all with her. I see it in Dai when he builds intricate and detailed ships and cranes and vehicles, or brews a pumpkin ale, or takes apart a truck engine. I see it in the Spud, when with simple words and elaborate gestures he tells me that a giant stole his nose, or cries because I ate his imaginary sandwich (oops). You cannot market that. You cannot sell it.

We are taught as we grow older that we should not make things up, and we lose the value of stories, and thus our imaginations. But what a bleak world we would have without them. It is part of our humanity, and I believe that as we change our society to adapt to a changing climate, when we all have to buy less whether we like it or not, we may well end up with a cultural shift back to telling stories around the fire, to making music together, to making things with our own hands and taking pride in that. Maybe then more of us will find faeries at the bottom of our gardens, or start talking to goddesses.

By far the most wonderful and important change in my life has been in how I perceive the landscape and how I relate to it. I have always wanted to experience magic, but from my teens onwards I have lived with my face in my smartphone and my mind full of wish lists – essentially the psychic equivalent of walking around with my eyes tight shut and my fingers in my ears, going "La la la...". The non-human world responded to me once I began to notice it and interact with it, in very real and undeniable ways.

So, where will I go from here? I have reduced my consumption by half in some areas, and more than that in others, but I'm aware that I can still do better. I have no intention of returning to my former, mindless spending habits, or excessive use of screens, which were as damaging to my soul as to my finances. I plan to continue in my current trajectory – to shop, spend and waste less, and thereby to live more lightly, freely and magically with each passing day.

Conclusion

As you can see from my story, the huge grinding engines of consumer society are fed on our insecurities. They profit from our comparison, our bad body image, our desire to be the perfect parent. They take our fears and our anxieties, and they spin them into profit for the one per cent, varying degrees of hardship for all the rest, and wholesale destruction of the very systems we and all other life rely on for our continued existence. It is my belief that Druidry offers a valuable alternative, in a time when society is looking for urgent solutions to the problems we have created with our endless desire for more.

Our current mode of living is presented as the pinnacle of human existence, yet by and large even in the wealthy West we are not happy. In the midst of extravagant abundance and the luxury of privilege, our well-being is suffering. Mental health problems are rising almost as relentlessly as the GDP. Further proof, if it were needed, that a life based on constant, limitless consumption may look good on Instagram, but it is not the good life. What good life could be built on a foundation of destruction and of suffering?

We are losing touch with our communities and with each other. I can see that it is valuable to be able to Skype our relatives in Hong Kong whilst we are living in Reading, but in an age of dawning climate chaos it is of utmost importance to turn our attention to our physical communities. We don't choose our neighbours. We may not even have chosen our home towns. But soon it may be more than necessary for us to pull together with those physically closest to us in order to build communities that are capable of surviving a changing world.[62]

Historically, the roles of the Druid – at varying grades – included bard, priest, arbitrator, diviner. These are relevant roles we can offer to our communities as we move forward, through and beyond the Anthropocene. We do not have to be clergy to offer support, guidance, practical help in whatever ways we are able. We can take for our examples Cat Treadwell in *A Druid's Tale*[63] and Emma Restall Orr in *Spirits of the Sacred Grove: The World of A Druid Priestess*.[64]

I would further suggest that the role of the Druid in this era of change include a new title: activist. This need not mean taking to the streets with a placard and megaphone – although it can, I try to join in with environmental protests and climate marches whenever I can – but could simply mean engaging with campaigns through social media or by email, or speaking to brands, businesses, councils and politicians to tell them what we want to see happen (and what we don't). Regardless of how we choose to act I feel we must do so – to be in active relationship with the earth should also mean to care for it and protect it, even – especially – in light of how much irreversible damage has already been done. I find it hard to see a future for a modern Druidry that does not engage with the world *as it is today*, even though that means facing up to some harsh truths about our situation and its causes.

Considering the idea of service to my community has helped me to become more vocal and active in local issues as well as global – I recently supported a successful campaign in my area to prevent the building of an incinerator in an area of natural beauty that provided a habitat to several endangered species of wildlife.

But service to a community need not always be dramatic or large-scale. On a personal level, we can offer support and help to those we know. For example, new mums and their partners often struggle to do the work of three people in a two-adult household (running a home, caring for a newborn, and earning a living), and would benefit from someone to sit with the baby for an hour so Mum can have a bath, or a nap. I have seen amongst my friends that new parents will rarely ask for this help, as we are so conditioned to the idea that all our needs can and should be fulfilled within the nuclear family. By taking the time to help each other in ways like this, we can strengthen our interpersonal relationships, our communities, and in small and quiet ways, begin to build a better way of living.

To provide another very simple example, during lockdown several of my friends and I who love to read set up a book group, whereby we could swap and share books amongst ourselves, either to keep or as a loan. This facilitated sharing of resources, something I feel is vitally important, but also gave us a space to chat, to exchange recommendations and stories, to take time for each other.

The goal of many modern paths, faiths and self-help philosophies is transcendence, enlightenment or personal development. Druidry offers a different way of looking at spirituality – not 'how can this benefit me', but 'what can I give'?

The myths that underpin Druidry generally emphasise generosity, hospitality and honour, which are radically different to our current capitalist values of accumulation, individualism and profit.

Druidry, and the mythopoetic worldview, gives us a different way of relating to other life. Above all I think it is time for us to remember that the world was not put here for our entertainment. Humans have made ourselves the centre of the web, expanding our societies, our cities, our roads, our farmlands, our monoculture crops as though we are the only beings who matter. All other life on Earth is forced to fit around the margins of our existence.

We often see ourselves as separate from nature. Particularly in our human-made landscapes we do not always remember to see the changing moods of the sky, the moon in all her phases, the wild animals who have adapted their ways of living to dwell beside and around us. The weather is at best a talking point, at worst a nuisance; the sun, wind or rain may not have chance to touch our skin. We have forgotten that, even with all our modern technology and ideals of progress, we still rely on trees for our air, and sun, rain, soil and pollinators for our food. We talk about 'saving the planet' as though it were an entirely abstract concept. As if the planet were optional and we could somehow go on without it.

We also see ourselves as separate from each other. This is why we do not rise up in outrage when we hear about the exploitation of garment workers, the children and prisoners of war working in open-pit mines to extract minerals to build PlayStations,[65] the fossil fuel companies funding militias to murder troublesome indigenous villagers.[66] The suffering is kept at a distance – we do not see it, we do not acknowledge it, we can ignore what makes us uncomfortable. There are no visible bloodstains on our sweatshop-made clothes.

We do not need to transcend this. We need to face it, and work to change it. The first thing we can change is ourselves.

About the Author

Katrina Townsend is becoming the anarchist hedge Druid she was born to be, exchanging shopping addiction and an Instagram obsession for green and simple living, creativity and connection with nature. Books are her lifelong passion, and other things that make her heart beat faster include folklore, folk art, folk rock (and pirate metal), libraries, forests, truck stops and other underrated liminal places, road ghosts, real ale, horned gods, yoga, yarn crafts, zines, mead and sunsets. In her former life as a goth blogger with over 10,000 followers, Kat previously contributed to Mookychick and Carpe Nocturne magazine. Living in England, she is mother of one small Spud, and married to a Welsh Viking. There are faeries at the bottom of her garden.

Notes

1. McGagh, M. (2018), *The No Spend Year: How You Can Spend Less and Live More*. London: Coronet.

2. Boyle, M. (2011), *The Moneyless Man: A Year of Freeconomic Living* (2nd ed.), London: Oneworld Publications.

3. Flanders, C. (2018), *The Year of Less: How I Stopped Shopping, Gave Away My Belongings and Discovered Life Is Worth More Than Anything You Can Buy In A Store.* Carlsbad: Hay House, Inc.

4. As time went on, I tweaked these rules several times. At one point I read *The Buy Nothing, Get Everything Plan* (Clark, L. and Rockefeller, R. (2020), New York: Atria Books) and decided that supporting artists was important enough to allow purchases of art and music as long as it was directly from the artist. Some months later, I realised that 'art' was a loose term that could encompass almost anything up to and including clothing, and that I was running out of room to hang prints. I still think it's a good loophole if unlike me you have the common sense to apply it sparingly and not attempt to shoehorn it into the monthly budget.

   In 2021 I tried a low-buy year, where I could make one 'allowed' purchase per month. This lasted until March, when I went on a crazy spending binge because I was frightened that the things I wanted to buy in future months might sell out or otherwise become unavailable. It also increased my focus on the accumulation of material things, which kind of defeated the whole point of the exercise.

   Currently (autumn 2021 at time of writing) I'm running a shopping ban with my original rules, though I may make possible exceptions for second-hand items later on in the year.

5. This, apparently, is of utmost importance to my generation.

Expedia conducted a survey that found that the priority for millennials when booking a holiday is how Instagrammable the location is. (Ritschel, C., The Independent (2017), *Millennials when booking holidays think of Instagram photos above all other factors*. Available at: https://www.independent.co.uk/life-style/millennials-holiday-decision-instagram-photos-factors-think-first-social-media-a8131731.html. Accessed 5th October 2021).

6. *The True Cost* (2015) Directed by: Andrew Morgan. Available at: Amazon Prime. Accessed: 5th October 2021.

7. BBC (2014), *Cambodia garment workers killed in clashes with police*. Available at: https://www.bbc.co.uk/news/world-asia-25585054 Accessed: 5th October 2021.

8. The collapse of the Rana Plaza factory complex in Dhaka, Bangladesh was to date the largest and deadliest disaster in the history of the fashion industry (although certainly not the first, and probably not the last given that very little has changed since). On 24th April 2013, the building crumbled – 1,134 people were killed and thousands more were injured. Workers in the garment factories had indicated cracks in the building to managers the day before but were told to return to work nonetheless, although other businesses in the complex such as shops and banks had been evacuated. Twenty-eight global brands were found to have been using the factories to manufacture their clothing, including Primark, Mango, Matalan, Benetton and Wal-Mart. By March 2014, only seven of those brands had contributed to the compensation fund for families of the victims. (Wikipedia Contributors (no date), *2013 Dhaka garment factory collapse*. Available at: https://en.m.wikipedia.org/wiki/2013_Dhaka_garment_factory_collapse Accessed: 5th October 2021.)

9. Wiseman, E., The Guardian (2019), *Are crystals the new blood diamonds?* Available at: https://www.theguardian.com/

global/2019/jun/16/are-crystals-the-new-blood-diamonds-the-truth-about-muky-business-of-healing-stones Accessed: 5th October 2021.

10. Slade, R., Yoga Journal (2020), *Is Your Palo Santo Habit Hurting the Environment?* Available at: https://www.yogajournal.com/lifestyle/palo-santo-ethics/ Accessed: 5th October 2021. White sage is also popularly used as a cleansing herb, but like Palo Santo, more writers are now raising awareness that these plants are sacred to communities of indigenous peoples and should not be used for commercial profit. (Moore, E., Triluna Wellness Blog (2019), *White Lies, White Sage: The Truth Behind Endangered Plants and Their Sacred Rituals*. Available at: https://www.trilunawellness.com/triluna-blog/2019/10/26/white-lies-white-sage-the-truth-behind-endangered-plants-amp-their-sacred-rituals Accessed: 5th October 2021.)

11. I feel like this probably doesn't actually need a footnote? But in case you've successfully avoided all popular media since the 2010s, Marie Kondo is the author of several wildly popular decluttering books and a Netflix series (and a manga) featuring her KonMari Method, in which you heap all your belongings in each category (clothes, books and so forth) into one pile and decide which to keep based on whether they 'spark joy'.

I've read all her books, including the seminal *Life-changing Magic of Tidying* (2014, London: Vermilion) (it's a folding masterclass), but the one I would probably most recommend is *Spark Joy* (2017, London: Vermilion). Whilst I've come to feel that extreme decluttering is not for me, and I'd like to see more emphasis on disposing of things responsibility if they don't spark enough joy, I do really appreciate the focus on caring for one's things, and of having *enough* – not an endless array of possessions.

12. Flanders originally documented her shopping ban, which

led her into minimalism and out of debt, on her blog under the name Blonde On A Budget (which I devoured). However most of her old posts and archives were deleted sometime circa 2020; when I went back to check for this reference, I discovered that she has since removed the blog entirely.

13. These were quite controversial when they appeared apparently. I have a horrible feeling that teenage me would have loved them. Ledbetter, C., Huffington Post (2017), *Topshop Wants You To Buy 'Mom Jeans' With Clear Plastic Kneecaps*. Available at: https://www.huffingtonpost.co.uk/entry/topshop-wants-you-to-buy-mom-jeans-with-plastic-kneecaps_n_58c6e47ee4b0598c66989745 Accessed: 5th October 2021.

14. Bowman, L., Metro (2017), *One in six young people won't wear an outfit again if it's been seen on social media*. Available at: https://metro.co.uk/2017/11/15/one-in-six-young-people-wont-wear-an-outfit-again-if-its-been-seen-on-social-media-7078444/ Accessed: 5th October 2021.

15. Morgan, M., Daily Mail (2015), *Throwaway fashion: Women have adopted a 'wear it once' culture, binning clothes after only a few wears (so they aren't pictured in same outfit twice on social media)*. Available at: https://www.dailymail.co.uk/femail/article-3116962/Throwaway-fashion-Women-adopted-wear-culture-binning-clothes-wears-aren-t-pictured-outfit-twice-social-media.html Accessed: 5th October 2021.

16. Benson, S., Grazia (2019), *Where Do Your Charity Shop Donations Really Go?* Available at: https://graziadaily.co.uk/fashion/news/charity-shop-clothes-donation/ Accessed: 5th October 2021.

17. Ricketts, L., Fashion Revolution Blog (2019), *Dead White Man's Clothes*. Available at: https://www.fashionrevolution.org/dead-white-mans-clothes/ Accessed: 5th October 2021.

18. Goldberg, E., Huffington Post (2016), *These African Countries Don't Want Your Used Clothing Anymore*. Available at: https://

www.huffingtonpost.co.uk/entry/these-african-countries-dont-want-your-used-clothing-anymore_n_57cf19bce4b06a 74c9f10dd6 Accessed: 5th October 2021.

19. Lawson, N., (2009), 'More' in *All Consuming* [Kindle version], Penguin Books. Available at: Amazon. Accessed: 5th October 2021.

20. Extinction Rebellion are "an international movement that uses non-violent civil disobedience in an attempt to halt mass extinction and minimise the risk of social collapse." Extinction Rebellion (2021), *About Us*. Available at: https:// extinctionrebellion.uk/the-truth/about-us/ Accessed: 6th October 2021.

21. I could no longer find this video, which featured XR spokesperson Clare Farrell, on the Extinction Rebellion website or YouTube channel (probably because it was part of their early 'Tell the Truth' campaign, which was intended to push leaders and governments to tell the truth about change and admit that we are in a climate and nature emergency. Which of course was successful, although sadly few of those in power seem to understand how to react to an emergency situation). So I went through XR's videos until I found the one I felt contained the most similar information, which was this one: Extinction Rebellion UK (2020), *Heading for Extinction and what to do about it | Dr Emily Cox | Extinction Rebellion*, 25th February. Available at: https://m.youtube.com/ watch?v=Jg3HCQ67qbY&t=2s Accessed: 6th October 2021.

22. I'm quite proud of being able to drop in a phrase like 'unmet needs', I feel like it really makes me sound like I've got my shit together. But actually, to give credit where credit is due, I learned this phrase – and all about how unmet needs were influencing my compulsive purchasing behaviour – from the workbook *To Buy or Not To Buy: Why We Overshop and How To Stop* (Benson, A. (2008), Boston: Trumpeter Books). And although I'm being fairly flippant

about it here, I did do the exercises from this workbook diligently and rigorously (and boy was it hard at times), and found them to be extremely beneficial.

23. Lane, J. (2001), *Timeless Simplicity: Creative Living in a Consumer Society*. Totnes: Green Books.

24. Hayes, S. (2010), *Radical Homemakers: Reclaiming Domesticity From a Consumer Culture*. Richmondville: Left To Write Press.

25. Gilbert, E. (2015), *Big Magic: How To Live A Creative Life and Let Go of Your Fear*. London: Bloomsbury.

26. Blackie, S. (2018), *The Enchanted Life: Unlocking the Magic of the Everyday*. Tewkesbury: September Publishing.

27. Goddess House is "a sacred healing temple in the heart of Glastonbury. Created by the Glastonbury Goddess Temple, we offer a loving, Goddess-inspired space where you can receive natural healing therapies." Goddess House Healing (2020), homepage. Available at: https://glastonburygoddesshouse.co.uk/ Accessed: 6th October 2021.

28. National Trust (no date), *The History of Glastonbury Tor*. Available at: https://www.nationaltrust.org.uk/glastonbury-tor/features/the-history-of-glastonbury-tor Accessed: 6th October 2021.

29. National Trust (no date), *Legends of the Tor*. Available at: https://www.nationaltrust.org.uk/glastonbury-tor/features/legends-of-the-tor Accessed: 6th October 2021.

30. McMillan, A. (no date), Glastonbury Tor – That Strange Hill, *Magical Mystery Tor: Legends, Folklore and Strange Experiences Around Glastonbury Tor*. Available at: https://glastonburytor.org.uk/mysterytor.html Accessed: 6th October 2021.

31. Jones, K. (no date), In The Heart of the Goddess, *The Goddess in Glastonbury [online version, originally written 1990]*. Available at: https://kathyjones.co.uk/the-goddess-in-glastonbury/ Accessed: 6th October 2021.

32. Martin, C. (2013), Fairy Room, *Myths and Legends of the Glastonbury Tor*. Available at: https://fairyroom.com/2013/04/myths-and-legends-of-the-glastonbury-tor/ Accessed: 6th October 2021.
33. I'm not affiliated in any way; I just think they're great bras.
34. The Druid Network (no date), *What Do Druids Do?* Available at: https://druidnetwork.org/what-is-druidry/beliefs-and-definitions/faq/druids/ Accessed 6th October 2021.
35. https://druidry.org/ Accessed: 6th October 2021.
36. Tiffany Aching is a young witch in Terry Pratchett's wonderful Discworld series (and also my favourite of his characters). She "appears to have a symbiotic, spiritual link with the hill lands on which she lives, and as such has shown herself to be strongly protective of the region and all its inhabitants." – Discworld Wiki contributors (no date), *Tiffany Aching*. Available at: https://discworld.fandom.com/wiki/Tiffany_Aching Accessed: 6th October 2021.
37. My favourite explanation of the mythopoetic worldview and the imaginal world comes from Sharon Blackie's website and is available here: https://sharonblackie.net/the-mythic-imagination-2/ (Accessed: 7th October 2021). To briefly (and clumsily) summarise, the mythopoetic worldview posits humankind as part of nature, but not nature as the inert collection of resources that is presented to us by capitalist industrialised society. This is a vibrant and animist view of the world, accepting not just the existence of our physical world but spirits, cosmic forces and the possibility of Otherworlds, as well as the anima mundi, or world soul. The mythopoetic worldview also suggests that mythic themes and archetypes are active within our lives and within the world itself.

It gets very Jungian, and whilst I don't accept that spirits, gods and so forth exist only as archetypes and not as individual entities, I certainly believe that a view of the biosphere and everything within it as alive, sentient and potentially communicative is more conducive to the future of human existence than our current anthropocentric way of life. I also strongly assert the importance of imagination and the imaginal world, which we are so often told is something to 'grow out of'.

38. For example, the formidable witch Granny Weatherwax is full of disdain for 'buying magic', and is exasperated at the importance given to stars, circles, wands etc., describing them as 'toys and decorations'. The point of witchcraft, she says, is helping people. *A Hat Full of Sky*, Pratchett, T. (2004), London: Random House, p. 251. (I always hoped to grow up into Granny Weatherwax, but it's frankly becoming apparent that I'm going to be more of a Nanny Ogg.)

39. Billington, P. (2011), *The Path Of Druidry: Walking the Ancient Green Way*. Woodbury: Llewellyn.

40. Billington, P. (2011), *The Path Of Druidry: Walking the Ancient Green Way*. Woodbury: Llewellyn, p. XXIII

41. https://www.1000hoursoutside.com/ Accessed: 9th October 2021.

42. Department for Environment, Food and Rural Affairs (2021), *Nature for people, climate and wildlife [Policy paper]*, para. 8. Available at: https://www.gov.uk/government/publications/nature-for-people-climate-and-wildlife/nature-for-people-climate-and-wildlife Accessed: 9th October 2021.

43. Hobson, S. (no date), *Is this the future of UK nature?* Available at: https://www.wwf.org.uk/future-of-UK-nature Accessed: 9th October 2021.

44. Friends of the Earth (no date), *More trees please: Why we need to double UK tree cover*. Available at: https://friendsoftheearth.uk/trees Accessed: 9th October 2021.

45. https://druidnetwork.org/ Accessed: 9th October 2021.

46. https://www.druidry.co.uk/ Accessed 9th October 2021.1

47. Billington, P. (2011), *The Path Of Druidry: Walking the Ancient*

Green Way. Woodbury: Llewellyn, p.43.

48. Weatherstone, L. (2015), *Tending Brigid's Flame: Awaken to the Celtic Goddess of Hearth, Temple and Forge* (Woodbury: Llewellyn).

49. Cabot, L. (1989), *Power of the Witch.* New York City: Delacorte Press.

50. Author unknown, Caera (ed.) (no date), The Nexus Druids, List of Druid Gods and Goddesses. Available at: https://sites.google.com/site/nexusdruids/tomes-of-the-earth/advanced-topics/gods/godslist Accessed: 9th October 2021

51. Black, S.M. (no date), *Brigit*, para. 5 [Druid Goddess]. Available at: https://druidry.org/resources/brigid-2 Accessed: 9th October 2021.

52. The list we used is available here: https://www.brighid.org.uk/sites.html Accessed: 9th October 2021.

53. Daimler, M. (2014), *Fairy Witchcraft.* Alresford: Moon Books.
Daimler, M. (2016), *Fairycraft.* Alresford: Moon Books.
Daimler, M. (2017), *Fairies: A Guide to the Celtic Fair Folk.* Alresford: Moon Books.
Daimler, M. (2018), *Travelling the Fairy Path.* Alresford: Moon Books.

54. Sjoo, M. (no date), *St Non's Well, Pembrokeshire.* Available at: https://insearchofholywellsandhealingsprings.com/source-first-series-contents/st-nons-well-pembrokeshire/ Accessed: 9th October 2021

55. Black, S.M. (no date), *Brigit*, para. 2-3 [Lands of the Goddess]. Available at: https://druidry.org/resources/brigid-2 Accessed: 9th October 2021.

56. The Diderot effect is named after a French philosopher in the 1700s who ended up in debt after his new dressing gown drove him to replace the rest of his belongings – a new possession leads to a 'spiral of consumption' which leads one to want more new things. (Insights Café (no date), *Our Wants and Needs wrapped in a Scarlet robe: The Diderot Effect.*

Available at: https://insightscafe.org/the-diderot-effect-why-we-want-things-we-dont-need-and-what-to-do-about-it/ Accessed: 9th October 2021.

57. Johnson, B. (2016), *Zero Waste Home.* London: Penguin Books.

58. I discovered artist Corinne Loperfido when YouTube recommended me the following video: StyleLikeU (2019), *Living in a Van & Resisting The Man: Corinne Loperfido's Zero Waste Life*, 3rd September. Available at: https://m.youtube.com/watch?v=2MTwQgntBuY Accessed: 9th October 2021.

59. A book I can recommend on this subject is: O'Connor, S. and Spunt, A. (2010), *No More Dirty Looks*. Cambridge: Da Capo Lifelong Books.

60. I recently read a really interesting book about this – Thomas, L. (2019), *Just Eat It*. London: Bluebird.

61. At the moment I have two go-to gardening books: Fowler, A. (2008), *The Thrifty Gardener* (new ed.) London: Kyle Cathie, and Locke, A. (2021), *The Forager's Garden*. East Meon: Permanent Publications.

62. Sometimes the communities fostered through disaster are the strongest – see, for example, *A Paradise Built in Hell* (Solnit., R (2010), New York City: Penguin Random House USA).

63. Treadwell, C. (2012), *A Druid's Tale*. Alresford: Moon Books.

64. Restall Orr, E. (2014), *Spirits of the Sacred Grove: The World of a Druid Priestess* [Kindle edition], Moon Books. Available at: Amazon. Accessed: 9th October 2021.

65. Shachtman, N. (2008), *Inside Africa's 'PlayStation War'*. Available at: https://www.wired.com/2008/07/the-playstation-2/ Accessed: 9th October 2021.

66. Amnesty International (2018), *Investigate Shell for complicity in murder, rape and torture*. Available at: https://www.amnesty.org/en/latest/press-release/2017/11/investigate-shell-for-complicity-in-murder-rape-and-torture/ Accessed: 9th October 2021.

Further Reading

Anderson, Miranda (2019), *More Than Enough: How One Family Cultivated A More Abundant Life Through A Year of Practical Minimalism,* Live Free Creative Co.

Benson, April Lane (2008), *To Buy Or Not To Buy: Why We Overshop and How To Stop,* Boston: Trumpeter Books

Billington, Penny (2011), *The Path Of Druidry: Walking the Ancient Green Way.* Woodbury: Llewellyn

Blackie, Sharon (2018), *The Enchanted Life: Unlocking the Magic of the Everyday.* Tewkesbury: September Publishing

Boyle, Mark (2011), *The Moneyless Man: A Year of Freeconomic Living* (2nd ed.), London: Oneworld Publications

Bravo, Lauren (2020), *How To Break Up With Fast Fashion,* London: Headline Home

Briggs, Raleigh (2009), *Make Your Place: Affordable, Sustainable Nesting Skills,* Portland: Microcosm Publishing

Brown, Nimue (2019), *Druidry and the Future,* independently published

de Castro, Orsola (2021), *Loved Clothes Last: How the Joy of Rewearing and Repairing Your Clothes Can Be a Revolutionary Act,* London: Penguin Life

Chivers, Jill (2020), *Shop Your Wardrobe: How a year without shopping helped me find myself and my authentic style… and how you can shop less and have more style too* [Kindle edition], Safari Group Publications

Dunn, Claire (2021), *Rewilding the Urban Soul: Searching for the Wild in the City,* London: Scribe

Gilbert, Elizabeth (2015), *Big Magic: How To Live A Creative Life and Let Go of Your Fear,* London: Bloomsbury.

Hayes, Shannon (2010), *Radical Homemakers: Reclaiming Domesticity From a Consumer Culture,* Richmondville: Left To Write Press

Hibbert, Katharine (2010), *Free: Adventures On The Margins Of A Wasteful Society*, London: Ebury Press

Hodgkinson, Tom (2007), *How To Be Free*, London: Penguin Books

van der Hoeven, Joanna (2019), *The Book of Hedge Druidry: A Complete Guide For The Solitary Seeker*, Woodbury: Llewellyn

Kelly, Kath (2018), *How I Lived A Year On Just A Pound A Day* [Kindle edition], independently published

Kindred, Glennie (2013), *Letting in the Wild Edges*, East Meon: Permanent Publications

Berners-Lee, Mike (2019), *There Is No Planet B: A Handbook for the Make or Break Years*, Cambridge: Cambridge University Press

Lane, John (2001), *Timeless Simplicity: Creative Living in a Consumer Society*. Totnes: Green Books.

Leonard, Annie (2010), *The Story of Stuff: How Our Obsession with Stuff is Trashing the Planet, Our Communities and Our Health – and a Vision for Change*, New York: Free Press

MacKinnon, J.B. (2021), *The Day The World Stops Shopping: How Ending Consumerism Gives Us A Better Life and A Greener World*, London: The Bodley Head

O'Driscoll, Dana (2021), *Sacred Actions: Living the Wheel of the Year through Earth-Centred Sustainable Practices*, Atglen: Red Feather

Ormerod, Katherine (2018), *Why Social Media Is Ruining Your Life* [Kindle edition], London: Cassell

Palmer, Amanda (2014), *The Art of Asking, or How I Learned to Stop Worrying and Let People Help*, London: Piatkus

Pike, Signe (2010), *Faery Tale: One Woman's Search For Enchantment In A Modern World*, London: Hay House

Pratchett, Terry (2004), *A Hat Full of Sky*, London: Doubleday

Price, Catherine (2018), *How To Break Up With Your Phone* [Kindle edition], London: Trapeze

Reddy, Jini (2020), *Wanderland: A Search For Magic In The Landscape*, London: Bloomsbury

Rees, Anuschka (2019), *Beyond Beautiful: A practical guide to being happy, confident, and you in a looks-obsessed world*, Berkeley: Ten Speed Press

Robin, Vicki and Dominguez, Joe (2008), *Your Money or Your Life: 9 Steps to Transforming Your Relationship with Money and Achieving Financial Independence* [2018 Revised ed.], New York: Penguin Books

Sanchez, Tara (2021), *Urban Faery Magick: Connecting to the Fae in the Modern World*, Woodbury: Llewellyn

Talboys, Graeme (2011), *The Druid Way (Made Easy)*, Alresford: O Books

Thompson, Christopher Scott (2016), *Pagan Anarchism*, Gods&Radicals

Valkyrie, Alley and Wildermuth, Rhyd (2016), *A Pagan Anti-Capitalist Primer*, Gods&Radicals

Weatherstone, Lunaea (2021), *Tending Brigid's Flame: Awaken to the Celtic Goddess of Hearth, Temple and Forge*, Woodbury: Llewellyn

Weber, Courtney (2015), *Brigid: History, Mystery and Magick of the Celtic Goddess*, San Francisco: Weiser Books

West, Asa (2020), *Five Principles of Green Witchcraft*, Gods&Radicals

Wolf, Naomi (1991), *The Beauty Myth*, London: Vintage

Wringham, Robert (2016), Escape Everything!: *Escape From Work, Escape From Consumerism, Escape From Despair* [Kindle version], London: Unbound

Blogs, Articles and Online Resources

Brown, Nimue, Druid Life blog, https://druidlife.wordpress.com/

The Druid's Garden blog, https://druidgarden.wordpress.com/

Frugalwoods blog, https://www.frugalwoods.com/

Grey, Peter (2014), *Rewilding Witchcraft*, Scarlet Imprint

van der Hoeven, Joanna, Down the Forest Path blog, https://downtheforestpath.com/

Mr Money Mustache blog, https://www.mrmoneymustache. com/

Restall Orr, Emma (The Druid Network), *A Perennial Course in Living Druidry*. Available at: https://druidnetwork.org/what-is-druidry/learning-resources/perennial/

Windling, Terri, Myth and Moor blog, https://www.terriwindling. com/blog/

MOON
BOOKS

PAGANISM & SHAMANISM

What is Paganism? A religion, a spirituality, an alternative
belief system, nature worship? You can find support for all these
definitions (and many more) in dictionaries, encyclopaedias, and
text books of religion, but subscribe to any one and the truth will
evade you. Above all Paganism is a creative pursuit, an encounter
with reality, an exploration of meaning and an expression of the
soul. Druids, Heathens, Wiccans and others, all contribute their
insights and literary riches to the Pagan tradition. Moon Books
invites you to begin or to deepen your own encounter, right here,
right now.
If you have enjoyed this book, why not tell other readers by
posting a review on your preferred book site.

Recent bestsellers from Moon Books are:

Journey to the Dark Goddess
How to Return to Your Soul
Jane Meredith
Discover the powerful secrets of the Dark Goddess and
transform your depression, grief and pain into healing
and integration.
Paperback: 978-1-84694-677-6 ebook: 978-1-78099-223-5

Shamanic Reiki
Expanded Ways of Working with Universal Life Force Energy
Llyn Roberts, Robert Levy
Shamanism and Reiki are each powerful ways of healing; together,
their power multiplies. *Shamanic Reiki* introduces techniques to
help healers and Reiki practitioners tap ancient healing wisdom.
Paperback: 978-1-84694-037-8 ebook: 978-1-84694-650-9

Pagan Portals – The Awen Alone
Walking the Path of the Solitary Druid
Joanna van der Hoeven
An introductory guide for the solitary Druid, *The Awen Alone* will
accompany you as you explore, and seek out your own place
within the natural world.
Paperback: 978-1-78279-547-6 ebook: 978-1-78279-546-9

A Kitchen Witch's World of Magical Herbs & Plants
Rachel Patterson
A journey into the magical world of herbs and plants, filled with
magical uses, folklore, history and practical magic. By popular
writer, blogger and kitchen witch, Tansy Firedragon.
Paperback: 978-1-78279-621-3 ebook: 978-1-78279-620-6

Naming the Goddess
Trevor Greenfield
Naming the Goddess is written by over eighty adherents and
scholars of Goddess and Goddess Spirituality.
Paperback: 978-1-78279-476-9 ebook: 978-1-78279-475-2

Shapeshifting into Higher Consciousness
Heal and Transform Yourself and Our World with Ancient
Shamanic and Modern Methods
Llyn Roberts
Ancient and modern methods that you can use every day to
transform yourself and make a positive difference in the world.
Paperback: 978-1-84694-843-5 ebook: 978-1-84694-844-2

Readers of ebooks can buy or view any of these bestsellers by
clicking on the live link in the title. Most titles are published in
paperback and as an ebook. Paperbacks are available in traditional
bookshops. Both print and ebook formats are available online.

Find more titles and sign up to our readers' newsletter at
http://www.johnhuntpublishing.com/paganism
Follow us on Facebook at https://www.facebook.com/MoonBooks
and Twitter at https://twitter.com/MoonBooksJHP